YOUR LEADERSHIP
BLUEPRINT
FOSTERING PSYCHOSOCIAL
SAFETY AT WORK

DR. MICHELLE MCQUAID & DR. PAIGE WILLIAMS

Your Leadership Blueprint: How to Foster Psychosocial Safety at Work

Authors: Michelle McQuaid and Paige Williams
PO Box 230 Albert Park, VIC, 3206 Australia
ABN: 88094250503

www.michellemcquaid.com
Email: chelle@michellemcquaid.com

ISBN: 978-0-9872714-9-5

Design and typesetting: Michelle Pirovich www.thesqueezebox.com.au
Editing: Carla Ford, Julie Weste, Shirley-Moana Duff, Simone Outteridge, Helen Vatzakis

For the leader in each of us who knows there is a way to lead that supercharges safety, wellbeing, and performance. We hope this book helps you turn this knowing into reality for you and your teams.

Contents

INTRODUCTION

WHY LEADING OTHERS IS HARD

"I've learned that people will forget what you said, people will forget what you did, but people will never forget how you made them feel."

~ Maya Angelou

Leading a team of people has never been an easy task. While popular management theories would like us to believe that people can be controlled like machines, this is rarely the reality experienced by most leaders. Instead, as we try to motivate our team towards achieving a common goal, we tend to repeatedly discover that the way each person thinks, feels, and acts is complex, dynamic, diverse, and often surprising.

As a result, studies have found that the most successful leaders no longer waste time and energy trying to "manage" the motivation, engagement, and commitment of others. Instead, they "care" about their people and continuously invest in building a culture where their team thrives, even when the work is challenging. For example, as Professor Linda Hill's longitudinal research on leaders who have the most positive impact notes: "Instead of being at the front of the stage, showing others the way, these leaders learned to set the stage and create an environment in which others were willing and able to do the hard work of innovation."

As many organizations and systems change researchers have observed, trying to "manage" a living system – such as your team – by imposing rigid structures and using promises of rewards or threats of punishment to solve complex challenges is a fool's errand. You may secure begrudging compliance to the tasks you require of them, but you'll be unlikely to win their ongoing commitment.

In fact, Margaret Wheatley, author of the widely acclaimed *Leadership and the New Science*, cautions: "If we believe that there is no order to human activity except that imposed by the leader, that there is no self-regulation except that dictated by policies, if we believe that responsible leaders must have their hands into everything, controlling every decision, person, and moment, then we cannot hope for anything except what we already have – a treadmill of frantic efforts that end up destroying our individual and collective vitality."

This may help to explain why in May 2019, the World Health Organization classified burn-out as a workplace phenomenon resulting from chronic workplace stress that has not been successfully managed. And, why a growing list of countries are advocating – and in some cases regulating – for workplaces to proactively address the psychosocial (emotional and social) hazards related to both job demands (workplace factors that cause stress) and job resources (workplace factors that protect from stress).

Unfortunately, leading a culture of safety and care that supports people's mental health and wellbeing is a set of skills still rarely taught in most leadership training programs. This book brings together decades of research and experience in workplaces to put the latest science at your fingertips. We'll help you to:

- **Part I: Build Literacy** – We'll start by reviewing your rapidly evolving psychosocial safety leadership responsibilities, so you have a better sense of what is required. Then, we'll introduce you to the one, small, evidence-based action that can help lower all the psychosocial risks that teams experience. And, we'll provide you with simple language tools that can be tailored to your team, to help you have better conversations about the importance of safety and care as you work together.

- **Part II: Invest In Evaluation** – We'll help you assess the levels of safety and care in your team by providing you with quantitative tools to measure the levels of psychosocial risk, the leadership support you are providing, and the organizational support your workplace provides. We'll also supply you with qualitative tools to help you talk with your team about the risks they may be experiencing. And, most importantly, we'll show you how to identify what's working well, where you and your team may be struggling, and how you can learn and act on the data you've gathered.

- **Part III: Boost Activation** – Safety and care perceptions, experiences, and behaviours are diverse and have been found to spread through a complicated web of social connections in our workplaces at the "Me" (individual), "We" (leaders and teams), and "Us" (workplace) levels. There is not one strategy that works for everyone or for every team. So, we'll provide you with evidence-based toolboxes of small actions you can experiment with integrating into your existing ways of working to activate more psychological safety and care in your team.

- **Part IV: Sustain Determination** – Building a culture of safety and care is never a tick-and-flick compliance exercise. It takes an ongoing loop of feedback, learning, and adaptation as the world around your team continues changing. We'll help you map a "living plan" that can be integrated into your existing leadership and team practices to ensure you have the resources, support, and agility to care for your team's mental health and wellbeing, even when the work you're doing makes this challenging.

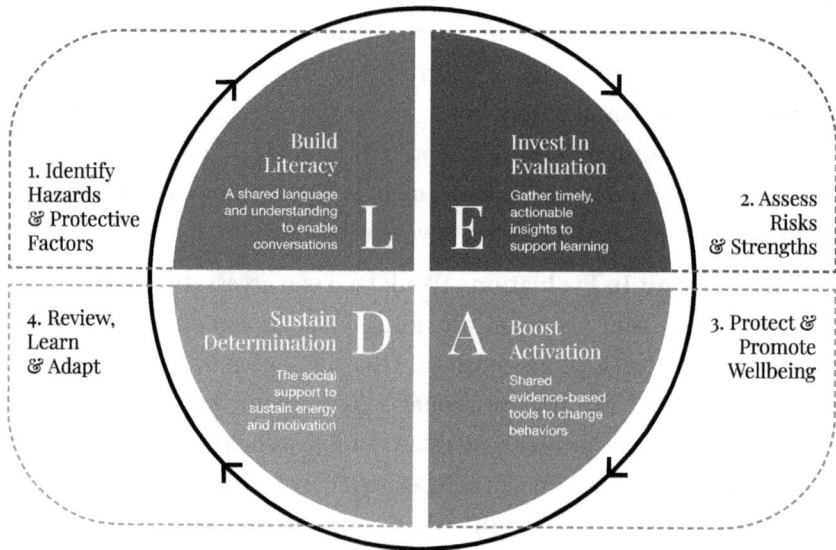

Figure 1: LEAD Framework

Along the way we'll provide you with plenty of real-world case stories to inspire you, and tools you can use to immediately apply what you're learning. If you can find a small group of peers (even one or two other leaders) to work through these steps together, you'll find this an easier and richer learning experience as you experiment and share your learnings with each other. Or, you may wish to share this journey openly with your team.

We do want to provide an important caution about the data that informs the steps in this book. Good science is never "proven"; it is always unfolding as it tests and challenges old ideas and seeks new explanations. With this in mind, we encourage you to use the research throughout this book to accelerate your understanding, inspire your practices, and then pull these ideas apart as you experiment with what works best for you and your team when it comes to LEADing a culture of safety and care.

Let's begin.

PART I
BUILD
LITERACY

"The limits of my language are the limits of my world."

Ludwig Wittgenstein

Researchers suggest that when we lack the language to talk about what we're experiencing, we struggle to understand what is happening, to manage our emotions, and to ask for the help we need. This is because the words we use have a direct effect on our brain and bodies.

Neuroscientists have found that the regions our brains use to process language are the same regions that regulate our heart, lungs, metabolism, and immune system. As a result, the words we use with each other can move our heart rate up and down, adjust the amount of glucose entering our bloodstream, and change the flow of chemicals that support our immune system.

In addition, Dr. Brené Brown notes that the language we use is a portal to meaning-making, connection and learning that shapes the way we think, feel, and act. For example, depending on the dialect, Inuit Eskimos have many words to describe dimensions of "snow", which allows them to think about, feel about, and interact with snow in far more nuanced ways than the one English word provides.

To create a shared language of safety and care for your team, we need to explore what the latest research suggests and, in some cases, what the most recent codes or legislation requires. We also need to incorporate any existing mental health and wellbeing language, tools, and support that your team already confidently discuss.

To assist we've created a "Language Placeholder" for you to capture the phrases and words that might resonate most with your team. As you move through Chapters 2 and 3, we've included "Mindful Moments" to encourage you to pause, reflect, and add any phrases or words that will make it easier for your team to talk with each other about "safety" and "care" at work.

We've also provided an example of how you can use your "Language Placeholder" to draft your own "Language Framework" that can be co-created with your team. Inviting your team to help finalize this Framework is in itself an act of safety and care that will help to build your team's levels of literacy. So be sure not to miss this step!

You can download an editable PDF of the "Language Placeholder" to use as you read the next two chapters here: **www.theleaderslab.net/leadersblue printresources.**

Your Language Placeholder

	KEY WORDS
Safety Definition *What does safety mean for your team and in your workplace? Which hazards are your team facing?*	
Care Definition *What does care mean for your team and in your workplace? Do you have a framework to support mental health and wellbeing?*	
Our Context *What is the context in your team and workplace for building a culture of safety and care? Who is responsible?*	
Our Goal *What is the goal for supporting safety and care in your team and workplace? How will you measure your success?*	
Our Tools *What are the evidence-based tools your team and workplace want to prioritize to support safety, mental health and wellbeing?*	

KEY PHRASES	IDEAS/NOTES

Your Safety & Care Shared Language Framework Example

When it comes to building a shared language, we recommend keeping your words and phrases as simple, actionable, and easy to remember as possible. It is also important to ensure that your language does no harm to others. Language that excludes or assumes one person's truth is the same for everyone can unintentionally add to workplace stress. This is why we recommend building your shared framework with your team.

Use your "Language Placeholder" to share what you're learning about the importance of safety and care with your team. Then add and remove words and phrases from the example below or start with a completely blank page to build your shared dialect.

For example:

Safety Definition

We believe we are being mentally, socially, and physically protected from danger, risk, or injury as we work together.

Every job involves some psychosocial hazards. The way our work is designed, the social support available, our work conditions, and our work experiences can increase the risk of work-related stress and harm people's health. Minimizing these risks is in everybody's best interest.

Care Definition

We believe our mental, social, and physical wellbeing matters to others.

We all need to feel connected, competent, and free to make our own choices. When we prioritize small frequent actions of compassion, appreciation, responsibility and emotional wisdom (CARE) for each other, we improve psychological safety. Supporting these strengths help us to thrive, even when our work is challenging.

Our Context

Building a culture of safety and care is a shared responsibility.

We are all in this together. Our safety and care habits, attitudes and behaviours spread through a complicated web of social connections at the "Me" (individuals), "We" (leaders and teams), and "Us" (workplace) levels.

Our Goal

To learn together by asking questions, experimenting, and seeking and providing feedback.

Our feelings of safety and care at work ebb and flow because people are complex and the world in which we work is dynamic. We need to value what works and build on these strengths. When we find ourselves struggling, we need to remember it is an invitation to learn and grow and take action.

Our Tools

Small acts of care add up.

We are never "won-and-done" when it comes to safety and care. Weaving small actions of CARE into our current role modelling, routines, rituals and rules can have a big impact on protecting our mental health, promoting our wellbeing and supporting our performance.

CHAPTER 1

The Risks Of Psychosocial Hazards

Studies are clear that anything that contributes to chronic stress can gradually erode parts of our brains, cause illness in our bodies and make us more vulnerable to stress of all kinds. Unfortunately, even before the global pandemic, the rising incidence of mental health injuries in workplaces were starting to ring alarm bells. For example, in Australia between 2014 and 2018, there was a 53 percent increase in psychosocial injury claims. In contrast, physical injury claims grew by only 3.5 percent during the same period.

Not only that, the cost of psychosocial injuries to workplaces, insurers and governments were starting to skyrocket. In Australia, since 2017, workers' compensation claims relating to mental health have increased by an average of 22 percent each year, with the cost per person being approximately $85,000 and requiring 175 days off work. In contrast the cost of a physical injury per person was approximately $21,000 and required 44 days off work.

With the costs of psychosocial injuries and lost productivity starting to add up to billions of dollars each year in many countries, governments around the world have taken steps to provide workplaces with better guidance and greater accountability for the way they are caring for the mental health and wellbeing of their people. Which is why you've picked up a book now about addressing psychosocial hazards. So, what do you need to know?

The Burnout Phenomenon

Let's be clear, burnt out is more than simply feeling a bit stressed and tired because we're working on a big project or in the middle of the busy part of the year. The World Health Organization notes that the symptoms of burnout are experienced persistently over a prolonged period and are assessed by our levels of:

- **Exhaustion** – Feeling physically, mentally, and emotionally drained. Eventually, chronic exhaustion leads us to disconnect or distance ourselves emotionally and cognitively from our work to cope with the overload.

- **Cynicism** – Distancing ourselves from others at work. We start to become overly irritated by other people and see them as problems, rather than as people we may be able to help.

- **Inefficacy** – Feeling we are accomplishing nothing. We struggle to identify the resources available to support our work, and as it becomes harder to deliver results, we increasingly feel that our efforts are meaningless.

Burnout was first used as a term in the 1970s by psychologist Herbert Freudenberger after he observed people in helping professions increasingly becoming exhausted and detached from their work over time. In the following decades it came to be recognized as a growing problem in workplaces that affected people from all walks of life and in all types of occupations. And, studies have found it is most often experienced by people who were once highly engaged and impassioned by their work.

Often mistaken as a lack of self-care, burnout is actually caused by an ongoing imbalance between the demands of our job (the sustained effort and energy it takes to get the work done), and the resources available to us (the motivation, energy, freedom, learning and support). It can be triggered by a variety of factors, including an unreasonable workload, lack of control over one's work, lack of supervisor and colleague support, poor change management, unfair treatment at work, and poor work-life balance.

Fortunately, a sudden shift in the balance of our work demands and resources is unlikely to immediately cause exhaustion, cynicism, and inefficacy. Rather, feelings of burnout tend to progress along a spectrum as an ongoing imbalance between our job demands and resources begins to cause greater and greater levels of stress. It's important to be aware that unlike an "on/off" button, we can be experiencing burnout, without *being* burnt out.

Unfortunately, the seismic shifts in the way we work over the last three decades has made it increasingly challenging for leaders to try and balance the job demands and resources of their teams. For example, in the 1990s as teams were equipped with laptop computers and mobile phones, the boundaries around workloads and levels of job control became increasingly blurry.

Then, in the early 2000s, as the adoption of the internet and globalization spread, the pace of change dramatically increased. Rather than meeting the heightened uncertainty and volatility this created with "care", workplaces tried to teach their leaders to "manage" change, which led to feelings of a lack of supervisor support and poor change outcomes.

When the 2008 Global Financial Crisis hit, people felt pressured to work longer and harder to secure their financial future. Struggling to navigate an increasingly disruptive world, workplaces tended to take advantage of every unpaid hour of labor offered, which accelerated the decline of adequate reward and recognition and heightened the lack of fairness.

And then came the 2020 global pandemic. As local public health lockdowns forced people to work from home or onto war-like frontlines, the imbalance between job demands and resources skyrocketed, and we witnessed the highest levels of burnout ever recorded.

As a result, the context of how we work has been forever changed. The actions being taken by governments and workers since the pandemic are forcing many workplaces to put in place better protection for the mental health and wellbeing of their teams. So, what does this mean for us practically as leaders?

What Are Psychosocial Hazards?

Every job involves some psychosocial hazards that have the potential to harm people. What, how, when, where and with whom we work can create psychosocial risks due to deficiencies in the design, organization, and management of our work or a poor social context.

Most of us are exposed to a combination of psychosocial hazards as we go about our jobs. Listed below are many of the most common hazards identified in workplaces today.

Work Design Hazards

Psychosocial hazards can be related to the way people's work is designed and may include:

- **Lack of role clarity** – Not having a clear understanding of their role and responsibilities, can lead to feeling confused and frustrated.

- **Unachievable job demands** – Having too much work to do, or not having enough time to complete it, can lead to feeling stressed and anxious.

- **Low job control** – Having little control over their work, or a lack of decision-making power, can lead to feeling powerless.

- **Inadequate reward and recognition** – Not being valued or recognized for their contributions, can lead to feeling demotivated, underappreciated, and unimportant.

For Katie, a new primary school teacher, when the list of her school's requirements outside the classroom kept having "just one more thing" added to it, she found herself gradually working more and more unpaid hours to keep up. While she loved her work with the students, as weeks turned into months Katie found that the constant additions to her workload were leaving her feeling stressed, exhausted, and cynical about the way the school was caring for its teachers. Feeling unable to speak up about her workload and with no one at the school checking in to see if she needed support, eventually Katie's doctor signed a medical certificate for six weeks off work due to burnout. Katie never returned.

Social Support Hazards

Psychosocial hazards can also be related to people's interactions with others at work and may include:

- **Lack of supervisor support** – The absence of guidance, feedback, and emotional support provided by a supervisor, can lead to feeling isolated, insecure, and lacking direction.

- **Poor workplace relationships** – Lack of respect, trust, support and camaraderie among workers, leaders, and clients, can lead to unhealthy conflict and feeling isolated, reluctant to ask for help, and unable to do their jobs.

- **Bullying** – Repeated aggressive behaviour that involves the use of power or authority to harm or intimidate others. It can take many forms, including verbal, physical, and social aggression and can lead to feeling stressed, anxious, and afraid to go to work.

- **Harassment** – Discrimination that involves unwanted or inappropriate behaviour, such as sexual harassment or racial harassment, can lead to feeling stressed, anxious, and depressed.

For Hamil, who started their first job after completing Year 12 on a construction site, it was only a matter of months before their levels of stress felt overwhelming. Despite a helpful induction process, Hamil's supervisor was rarely available for conversations or meetings and hadn't once checked-in to see how Hamil was settling in. Their teammates were openly derogatory about Hamil's lack of experience, and they intentionally excluded Hamil from team social events on the premise that 'it's for lifers only'. Hamil needed this job, they wanted to find a way to make it work but didn't know who and how to ask for help, and in the meantime their stress levels continued to climb.

Work Condition Hazards

Psychosocial hazards can be related to the conditions under which people work and may include:

- **Poor change management** – Organizational changes that are not well thought out, planned, communicated, or executed, can lead to feeling confused, anxious, uncertain, and a lack of job insecurity.

- **Poor physical environment** – Being exposed to hazardous, unpleasant, or poor-quality environments and poorly maintained amenities (i.e., break rooms, meetings spaces, etc.) can evoke stress responses.

- **Remote or isolated work** – Work environments that are isolated from the assistance of other people and limit opportunities for interaction and support (i.e., working from home, working in rural or offshore locations, working non-typical work hours, working in an isolated area, or travelling a lot for work), can lead to a lack of clear boundaries, and feeling disconnected from others.

For Mark, his job as a social worker supporting adults with mental health challenges was the most meaningful part of his life. Every day he would get in his car and drive across his rural community to check-in with the people assigned to his care and see what support they may need. Mark found the hours of driving between appointments lonely and sometimes found himself alone in the homes of people who were really struggling, which could be very stressful.

After mentioning this to his supervisor, they agreed to use some of Mark's driving time each day to catch up by telephone on how he was doing, which clients he was seeing, and how his visits had gone. Mark was also provided with a panic alarm to alert his supervisor at the push of a button if he needed urgent support with a client and was reassured that if he had any concerns about visiting a client alone, his supervisor was happy to organize a colleague to attend with him. These actions helped Mark to feel less stressed about his work.

Work Experience Hazards

Psychosocial hazards can be related to people's experiences at work and may include:

- **Poor organizational justice** – Favoritism, lack of transparency in decision making, lack of equal opportunities, and lack of accountability can create a toxic work environment that undermines feelings of trust, commitment, and loyalty.

- **Violent and aggressive behaviours** – The use of force or the threat of force to harm or intimidate through the use of physical violence (i.e., hitting, pushing or throwing objects), verbal aggression (i.e., yelling, name-calling or threatening language), or psychological aggression (i.e., manipulation, intimidation or stalking) can cause fear, anxiety, and post-traumatic stress disorders.

- **Traumatic events and materials** – Physical or sexual assault, serious accidents, natural disasters, kidnapping or hostage situations, mass shootings, war and combat, terrorist attacks, and exposure to traumatic materials are life altering events that can have a serious impact on our wellbeing.

Melanie loved helping people in her role as an assistant in a large office supply retailer, but the recent addition of a new team member who was a close friend of the team supervisor, had changed their team dynamic for the worse. Despite clear guidelines about the fair distribution of shifts, Melanie found she was consistently being given late shifts without any consultation because the new member had to collect her children from school. After several months, Melanie raised the lack of fairness about shift allocations and her supervisor became defensive and responded aggressively. Melanie was left feeling shaken, uncomfortable, and reluctant to take any further action, while her stress about the lack of fairness in her team continued to fester and grow.

You can download this easy-to-follow poster to help you spot your team's psychosocial hazards at **www.theleaderslab.net/leadersblueprintresources**.

WORK DESIGN HAZARDS	**LACK OF ROLE CLARITY** Unclear understanding of role and responsibilities may cause confusion and frustration.	**UNACHIEVABLE JOB DEMANDS** Too much or too little work or not enough time for completion may cause stress and anxiety.
SOCIAL SUPPORT HAZARDS	**POOR SUPERVISOR SUPPORT** Lack of supervisor guidance, feedback and support may cause isolation, insecurity and lack of direction.	**POOR WORKPLACE RELATIONSHIPS** Lack of respect & support among workers, leaders & clients may cause conflict, isolation & inability to do the job.
WORK CONDITION HAZARDS	**POOR PHYSICAL ENVIRONMENT** Exposure to environmental hazards may cause physical and psychological health problems.	**POOR CHANGE MANAGEMENT** Poorly planned, communicated or executed organizational changes may cause confusion, anxiety and job insecurity.
WORK EXPERIENCE HAZARDS	**TRAUMATIC EVENTS** Life altering events can have a serious impact on our wellbeing.	**POOR ORGANIZATIONAL JUSTICE** Lack of transparency, equal opportunities and accountability may create a toxic work environment that undermines trust and commitment.

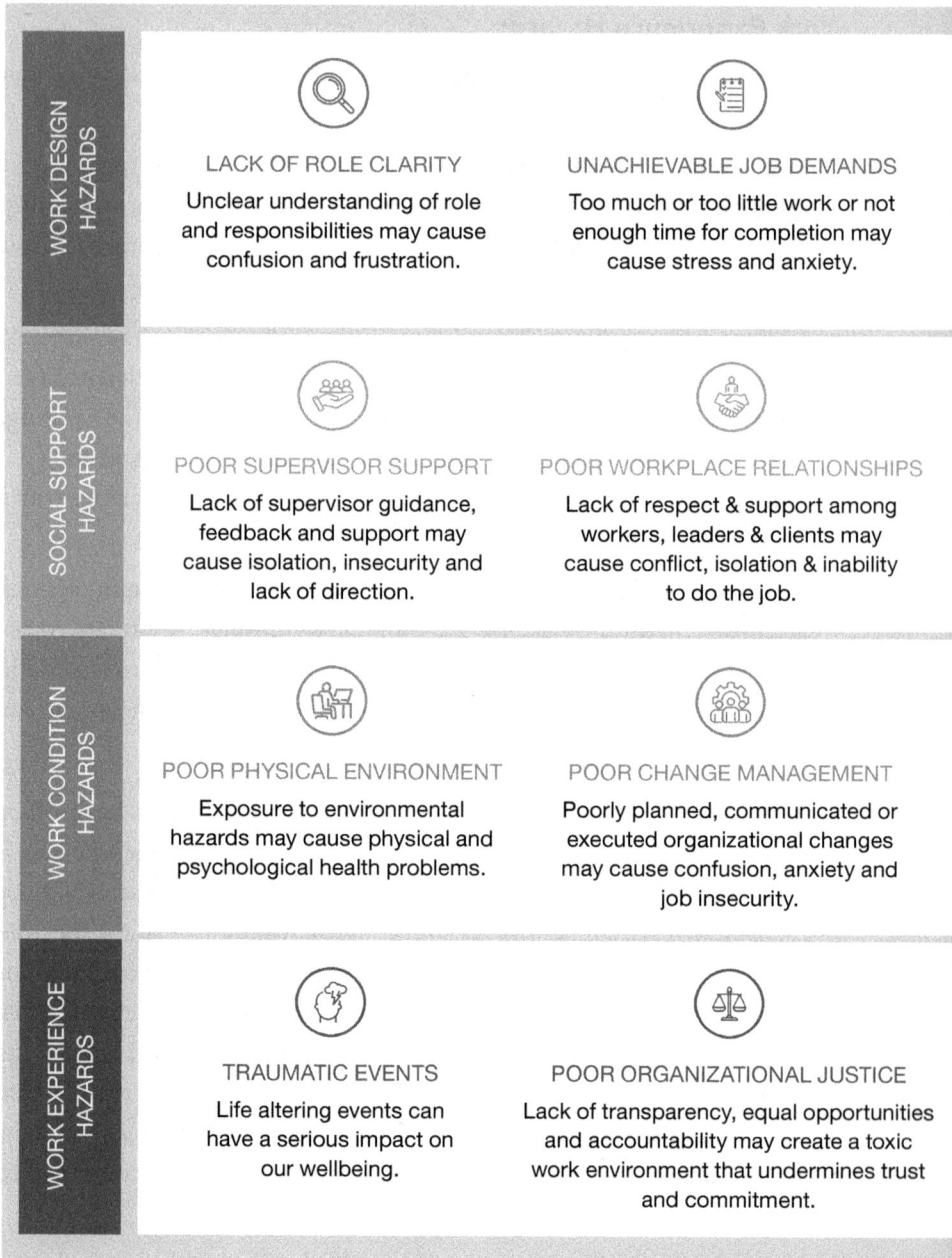

Figure 2: The Psychosocial Hazards

LOW JOB CONTROL

Little control over one's work or lack of decision-making power may lead to feeling powerless and frustrated.

INADEQUATE REWARD AND RECOGNITION

Not being valued or recognized may lead to feeling demotivated, under appreciated, and unimportant.

BULLYING

Repeated aggressive behavior that uses power or authority to harm or intimidate may include verbal, physical and social aggression.

HARASSMENT

Unwanted or inappropriate behavior, may cause feelings of stress, anxiety, and depression.

REMOTE OR ISOLATED WORK

Work in remote or isolated settings, without regular face-to-face interaction, may cause a lack of clear boundaries and feeling disconnection.

VIOLENT AND AGGRESSIVE BEHAVIORS

The use of force or threat of force to harm or intimidate may cause fear, anxiety, and post-traumatic stress disorders.

While we may each respond to the same hazards in different ways, the data suggests that these hazards can increase the risk of work-related stress, harm people's mental and physical health, and if prolonged, lead to burnout. Which is why workplaces are increasingly expected to do everything so far as is reasonably practicable to eliminate or at least minimize these risks.

> **Mindful Moment:** Are there any key words or phrases you want to add to your "Language Placeholder" to help your team define psychosocial hazards? Don't worry about listing all the hazards because next we'll help you assess ones specific to your team.

Psychosocial Hazards Around The World

As far back as 1984, the International Labour Organization and World Health Organization encouraged workplaces to start assessing and addressing psychosocial hazards. In 2018, a study of 132 countries found that 47 countries – most of them developed countries – had included mandatory psychosocial risk assessment and prevention in their national occupational safety and health legislation.

Then in 2021, the International Organization for Standardization (ISO), a worldwide federation of national standards bodies, published ISO 45003 – a voluntary standard designed to make workplaces psychologically safe and healthy. Created by representatives from 74 countries, the standard provides examples of what can be done to eliminate or manage psychosocial risks and support wellbeing.

In addition to these international efforts, many countries have established local standards and/or regulations that require workplaces to eliminate, or at least minimize as far as is reasonably practicable, psychosocial hazards. For example, lawyer Ellen Pinkos Cobb, in her book *Managing Psychosocial Hazards and Work-Related Stress in Today's Work Environment*, reports that in:

- **Nordic Countries & Belgium** – Local laws call for collaboration between employer, supervisors, and employees to establish a good working environment and take all precautions possible against the occurrence of sickness or accidents, including psychological injuries.

- **Europe** – In many European countries, the employer's duty of care is regarded as encompassing both the physical and psychological aspects of work. However, in 2021, the European Trade Union Institute (ETUI) called for an explicit EU Directive in the area of psychosocial risks in the workplace, as the degree to which psychosocial risks are included or explicitly mentioned in the legislation varies significantly between the Member States.

- **United Kingdom** – Employers are required to carry out an assessment of significant health and safety risks, including the risk of stress-related ill-health arising from work activities, and implement measures to control these risks. The U.K. Health and Safety Executive (HSE) Management Standards provide a systematic approach to implementing an organizational procedure for managing work-related stress.

- **Canada** – In 2013, Canada was the first country in the world to release a national standard for psychological health and safety in the workplace and provide a comprehensive set of voluntary guidelines, tools, and resources to implement its provisions, promote mental health, and prevent psychological harm at work. Canada's provinces are also now recognizing the importance of workplace psychological health and safety through their policies and laws.

- **The United States** – The Occupational Safety and Health Act (OSHA) has issued guidelines on preventing workplace violence and the Equal Employment Opportunity Commission (EEOC) has issued guidelines on preventing harassment and discrimination in the workplace. However, America is generally viewed as lagging behind other countries with minimal legislative support to protect workers' psychological health.

- **Mexico** – Comprehensive laws have been enacted to prevent mental health issues and psychological risk factors in the workplace. Employers are required to identify, analyze, and prevent work-related psychological risks that may harm employees' physical, social, and mental health.

- **Australia** – In 2021, Australia agreed to a series of substantive amendments to the model Work Health and Safety (WHS) Act, including express provisions dealing with psychological injuries. These amendments have now become law in most Australian states and territories.

- **Asia** – Many countries have laws and regulations in place, such as China's Occupational Safety and Health Management System – Requirements, which include provisions on addressing psychosocial hazards in the workplace. However, long working hours in most Asian countries remain a significant issue, resulting in occupational diseases and occasionally, sudden death.

- **Africa** – Many countries have laws and regulations in place, such as South Africa's Occupational Health and Safety Act (OHSA) or Ghana's Labor Act, which require employers to prevent and protect workers from work-related stress, violence, and harassment.

- **South America** – Many countries have laws and regulations in place, such as Brazil's Occupational Safety and Health Law (OSHL), which protect workers from psychosocial hazards and Argentina's Occupational Health and Safety Law, that requires employers to prevent and protect workers from work-related stress, violence, and harassment.

While penalties for non-compliance vary, based on the jurisdiction and the specific laws violated, they can include fines, imprisonment, and enforceable undertakings to take specific actions to address the non-compliance. For example, the High Court in Australia recently awarded a six-figure settlement to an employee due to the failures of their workplace to protect them from psychosocial harm. Unfortunately, even when psychosocial safety laws and regulations exist, they may not be enforced due to lack of local funding, political will, or organizational capacity.

What Are Leaders Responsible For?

Typically, the codes and legislation place the burden of responsibility on workplaces for creating psychosocially safe work environments. For example, Australian laws state that the primary responsibility rests with the Person Conducting a Business or Undertaking (PCBU) which includes employers, self-employed individuals, and in some case a volunteer or an employee who has some level of control over the work being carried out. However, in many organizations, the practical execution of these responsibilities tends to fall on the shoulders of leaders.

While the list of psychosocial hazards can vary by country, generally workplaces are encouraged – or in some cases required – to:

- **Identify and assess** the frequency, wellbeing impact, and duration of the wellbeing impact of psychosocial hazards.

- **Implement measures** to eliminate or control the identified hazards, where reasonably practicable.

- **Provide information, instruction, and training** to workers on how to recognize and manage the psychosocial hazards in their workplace.

- **Consult with workers and their representatives** on matters relating to psychosocial hazards and how they are managed.

- **Monitor the effectiveness of the controls** in place and make adjustments as necessary.

It is important to note that this is not an exhaustive list, that specific requirements vary depending on the nature of the work and the psychosocial hazards present, and that these regulations and standards are constantly evolving. This means every leader has a responsibility to themselves and their teams to understand what their duty of care comprises.

If your workplace has not provided you with information and training, then ask them for this support. Most of the regulations and standards clearly state that organizations must demonstrate a "leadership and management commitment to psychosocial safety". This means they must provide you with the knowledge, tools, and support to protect the mental health and wellbeing of your team.

Mindful Moment: Be sure to add any helpful key words or phrases from your research to your Language Placeholder.

Assessing Your Psychosocial Hazards

As each workplace and team experience different psychosocial hazards, the first step is to get clear on which hazards you need to be able to talk about, measure, and monitor with your team. Specifically, you're looking for experiences that may be considered unreasonable or excessive, and that are occurring frequently, over an extended period.

Assessment: Psychosocial Hazards Register

These hazards can often be identified using existing data, such as employee surveys, sick leave trends, workers' compensation claims, employee assistance data, formal grievances and complaints, exit interviews, industrial relations disputes, previous safety audits, and existing risk registers. Based on what you know from your data, which of the following hazards do you think your team frequently encounter for prolonged periods? Place a "Yes", "Maybe", or "No" in the column below and note any examples that come to mind.

You can download an editable PDF of the psychosocial hazards register to use as you read the next two chapters here: **www.theleaderslab.net/leaders blueprintresources.**

Hazards	Team Risk (Yes, Maybe, No)
Work Design	
Lack of role clarity: Not having a clear understanding of their role and responsibilities.	
Unachievable job demands: Having too much work to do or not having enough time to complete it.	
Low job control: Having little control over their work or a lack of decision-making power.	
Inadequate recognition and reward: Not being valued or recognized for their contributions.	
Social Support	
Lack of supervisor support: The absence of guidance, feedback, and emotional support.	
Poor workplace relationships: Lack of respect, trust, support and camaraderie among workers, leaders, and clients.	
Bullying: Repeated aggressive behaviour (verbal, physical and/or social) that involves the use of power or authority to harm or intimidate others.	
Harassment: Discrimination that involves unwanted or inappropriate behaviour, such as sexual harassment or racial harassment.	
Work Conditions	
Poor change management: Organizational changes that are not well thought out, planned, communicated or executed.	
Poor physical environment: Being exposed to environmental hazards such as noise, vibration, or chemical substances.	
Remote or isolated work: Working from a location outside of a traditional office setting, such as from home or from a remote location.	

Hazards	Team Risk (Yes, Maybe, No)
Work Experiences	
Poor organizational justice: Favoritism, lack of transparency in decision making, lack of equal opportunities, and lack of accountability.	
Violence and aggression: The use of force or the threat of force to harm or intimidate through physical violence, verbal aggression, or psychological aggression.	
Traumatic events or materials: Physical or sexual assault, serious accidents, natural disasters, hostage situations, mass shootings, war and combat, terrorist attacks or exposure to traumatic material.	
Other Hazards	
Examples	

Mindful Moment: Be sure to add the hazards you have marked "Yes" and any key words or phrases from your example to your "Language Placeholder".

Asking Your Team About Their Experiences

We also recommend – and sometimes the legislation requires – talking to your team about the hazards they are encountering. Every time you create a safe space for your team's voices to be heard and acted upon, the levels of safety in your team are likely to improve.

Unfortunately, we find leaders who have been focused on "managing" their team, tend to talk more than they listen. As a result, levels of safety in their team are often low and suddenly inviting people to speak up and share their psychosocial risks can feel like something they may be punished for later.

If speaking with candor and vulnerability is not the norm in your team yet, we suggest having a trusted independent facilitator guide these conversations. Based on what they know of you and your team, they may recommend this conversation is held with everyone together or that a series of individual discussions are held. Your willingness to allow your team to speak freely, without fear of threats or punishment, is a powerful way to demonstrate your commitment to their safety.

However, if your team is already comfortable providing feedback, asking questions, offering ideas, and speaking up about what's not working, then we suggest you lead this conversation by:

- Sharing why you're committed to building a culture of safety and care for your team (this is a great chance to introduce some of the language you are finding helpful);

- Setting an intention not to blame or shame each other, but to continue learning about how to work together safely;

- Acknowledging the psychosocial hazards you believe your team may be experiencing;

- Inviting reflections from team members about the hazards you've identified or others they are experiencing;

- Providing a clear sense of next steps to address these hazards together. This should include an invitation to help shape the shared language you'll use as a team to talk about these challenges and opportunities in future.

Remember, your goal is to speak less and listen more. Don't miss this opportunity to improve safety in your team.

> **Mindful Moment:** Be sure to add any key words or phrases from your conversation to your Language Placeholder.

Why Bother?

Protecting your team from psychosocial risks is not just a legal compliance issue, it is a business imperative. Studies have found that work-related stress and burnout can lead to:

- **Lower levels of engagement** – Gallup estimate disengaged staff cost $3,400 out of every $10,000 in salary they are paid.

- **Increased absenteeism** – Physical symptoms such as headaches, muscle pain and fatigue, and psychological symptoms such as depression and anxiety make people 63 percent more likely to take sick days.

- **Increased compensation claims and medical expenses** – A Stanford Graduate School of Business study found that workplace stress in America contributes to at least 120,000 deaths each year and accounts for up to $190 billion in health care costs.

- **Decreased productivity** – Researchers have found high levels of stress can temporarily impair strategic thinking, dull creative abilities, and make it hard to focus and complete tasks. It can also lead to an increase in mistakes, errors, and accidents. One study in 2017, of over 17,000 employees across 19 industries, suggested stress costs U.S. employers an estimated $500 billion dollars in lost productivity annually.

- **Lower levels of customer satisfaction** – When people experience higher levels of job stress and emotional exhaustion, studies have found they are more likely to engage in negative behaviours towards customers, such as being rude or dismissive, leaving customers more likely to have negative perceptions of the business and less likely to make repeat purchases.

- **Increased turnover** – People are nearly three times as likely to leave their jobs, which results in additional costs for recruiting and training new employees.

- **Litigation** – Legal fees, expert witness fees, discovery costs, and potential settlement or judgment costs can make the litigation of psychosocial hazards incredibly expensive. For example, an American federal jury awarded $168 million in damages to a former employee of a healthcare provider who alleged that she was subjected to severe and pervasive sexual harassment and discrimination on the job.

- **Reputational damage** – Workplaces that are seen as unresponsive or unwilling to address psychosocial hazards can suffer significant damage to their reputation and brand if these issues become public. For example, Uber's poor handling of sexual harassment and work design complaints have led to wide-spread media and social media criticism, 200,000 customers deleting their Uber accounts, large numbers of employee resignations, legal class actions, government investigations and a lack of stock market confidence.

To put these very real business challenges into perspective, researchers estimate that burnout costs U.S. employers around $300 billion each year.

And preliminary research shows that Australian businesses lose over $6.5 billion each year by failing to provide early intervention/treatment for their employees.

Psychosocial injuries also have a societal impact because psychosocial injuries have been found to be related to increased work-family conflict, family breakdown, suicide, abuse of medications and healthcare costs. In 2008, the annual cost to society (including the cost of mental healthcare, social service costs, and other costs) of work-related stress and stress-related illness in Canada, was estimated to be $2.75 billion for a low prevalence of stress, and $8.25 billion for higher estimated prevalence.

While the billion-dollar retailer Patagonia is known for its iconic outdoor clothing and gear, it has become renowned for its exceptional culture of safety and care. With more than 70 stores around the world and over 3,000 employees, Patagonia has always been clear that when it comes to achieving its mission of using business to inspire and implement solutions to the environmental crisis, there is a powerful connection between treating things as disposable, and treating the people who make those things as disposable.

When it comes to minimizing psychosocial hazards, Patagonia prioritizes:

- **Job demands** – A 9/80 work schedule that gives employees a three-day weekend every other week. Employees work nine hours a day from Monday through Thursday and eight hours on alternating Fridays. They get every second Friday off. In addition, scheduling meetings during lunchtime is forbidden because most people are out doing yoga or going for a jog.

- **Job control** – Flexible working, as long as the work gets done with no negative impact on co-workers. For example, employees are encouraged to take time off to do things that make them happy, like going surfing.

- **Reward and recognition** – Up to two months off, with pay, to volunteer with an environmental organization or project after employees have worked at the company for a year.

- **Supervisor support** – Empathy, understanding, and a listening strategy are prioritized by leaders to ensure employees' ideas and feedback are heard, and these insights are used to inform better decision making.

- **Workplace relationships** – A focus on having a "culture add" vs a "culture fit" for new hires. This means reading resumes from the bottom up to understand a candidate's interests and hobbies and to know whether they share a passion for the outdoors.

- **Discrimination** – A commitment to diversity of all kinds and specifically at least 50 percent of upper-management positions held by women.

- **Change management** – Regular town hall meetings to share what's going on and give employees visibility. Everyone is encouraged to speak up and challenge what's happening. This gives employees a platform to speak and be heard.

- **Physical environment** – Not even the founder has a private office as everyone works in open rooms with no separations.

Does it work?

Patagonia is regularly included on "best place to work" and "most loved companies" lists based on their employees' evaluations. The company has an enviably low employee turnover rate of only 4 percent (the retail and consumer product sector average is more than triple that at 13 percent). It has one of the of the best employee-attraction ratios of any company, averaging 900 applications for every one open position. And in 2022, the founder Yvon Chouinard and his family donated the company's non-voting stock, valued at $3 billion), to an American non-profit organization working for climate action and policy advocacy. Patagonia expects that, depending on the health of the business, company profits of $100 million will be donated to these causes each year.

While this is great for Patagonia, their employees and hopefully our planet, what does it mean for the language of safety and care you want to build for your team? Patagonia don't just talk about how they comply with the codes or legislation that impacts their business. Instead, they focus their language, conversations, and actions on demonstrating their commitment to caring for their workers. Their CEO even wrote a book for them about it.

How can you balance your language of safety compliance with your commitment to care for your people's mental health and wellbeing? Let's see what the science suggests.

CHAPTER 2

The Opportunity Of Psychological Safety

Psychosocial hazards arise from the ways we work together. When we strip back all the legal language, they are the emotional and social challenges found in how we connect, communicate, and support each other as we organize the completion of our work. And while identifying the hazards, assessing them, controlling them, and reviewing our efforts sounds logical, the danger of "managing" psychosocial risks lies in underestimating the complex and dynamic nature of the ways we work together.

For better or worse, the ways we work together are rarely logical. This is because our diverse personalities, values, life experiences, skills, job demands, and hopes make our relationships at work complex. Add to this our dynamic, always changing work environments, and even small changes such as an increased performance goal, a shortened deadline, or variations to your team, and we can dramatically increase the psychosocial risks we experience.

Clearly, doing everything "reasonably practicable" to eliminate or minimize psychosocial risks, as required by the legislation and codes, is never a "won-and-done" exercise but instead requires an ongoing commitment to learning how to safely navigate our complex relationships and dynamic workspaces together. So, what can we add to our shared language that might make the process of navigating psychosocial risks easier – especially given there are so many of them?

Why Learning To Be Safe Together Can Be Hazardous

The U.S. Surgeon General's workplace mental health and wellbeing framework notes: "People cannot perform well at work if they feel physically or psychologically unsafe." Why might this be the case? Because studies have found that our performance depends on our willingness to be vulnerable with each other as we collaborate and learn together. We need to be willing to ask questions, suggest new ideas, and own our mistakes to build our skills and improve our performance.

This type of learning requires us to take risks that can trigger our brain's threat systems. For example, studies have found that the fear of appearing foolish or incompetent in front of other people, causes our brains to respond in the same way as if we were experiencing physical pain. After all, if our boss or colleagues decide we're incompetent, we won't just feel the social pain of humiliation, exclusion, or rejection – we might lose our job. As a result, too often we believe the best way to protect ourselves is by saying nothing.

However, far from keeping us "safe", our reluctance to speak up at work means that we miss out on the learning opportunities to address what start out as small risks but over time can grow into big problems that can lead to severe stress and burnout. Fortunately, researchers have found that our brain's fear of learning alongside others can be overcome. The key is having what workplace researcher Dr. Amy Edmondson describes as "psychological safety".

What Is Psychological Safety?

More than sixty years of research has found that psychological safety has positive benefits for learning, performance, and wellbeing. Often defined as a "set of taken-for granted beliefs about how others will respond when we put ourselves on the line", psychological safety describes a team climate characterized by a blend of trust, respect, and care for each other.

DESIRED WORKPLACE OUTCOMES IN TEAMS	WHEN PSYCHOLOGICAL SAFETY IS FULLY PRESENT	WHEN PSYCHOLOGICAL SAFETY IS COMPLETELY ABSENT
Teams collaborate successfully because people trust and respect each other.	Team members communicate, solve problems, and make decisions effectively together.	Team members have strained commun- ication, and problems and conflicts are left unresolved.
Innovation and creativity are fostered so teams can adapt and improve over time.	Team members take calculated risks, try new things, and experiment with different approaches.	Team members are less willing to take risks or try new things and miss opportunities for improvement.
Diverse perspectives and candor are valued so people are confident to speak up.	Team members openly and honestly share their thoughts, ideas, and concerns.	Team members are hesitant to share their thoughts, ideas, or concerns openly.
Accountability is improved because teams have the permission to learn, grow, and develop their skills.	Team members ask questions, seek, and provide feedback, and admit to mistakes and failures.	Team members blame and criticize each other leading to defensiveness, hostility, and the punishment of mistakes.
Support for each other is provided which creates feelings of inclusion and belonging.	Team members willingly listen, share information, make introductions, offer help, and express appreciation for each other.	Team members compete for resources and feel disengaged and disconnected from each other.

Figure 3: Psychological Safety Continuum

For example, a longitudinal study by Google's People Analytics Unit identified psychological safety as the number one characteristic of its most successful teams. After combing through fifty years of academic findings and mapping data points about personality types, gender, education, skills, motivations, and social relationships across more than 100 teams, they found ... nothing. The 'who' part of a team's composition made no difference when it came to effectiveness.

Google went back to the drawing board and noticed that in other studies of teams, psychologists and sociologists often highlighted the importance of group norms – the traditions, unwritten rules, and behavioural standards that govern how a group functions. For example, Google found one engineer had told researchers that his team leader was "direct and straightforward, which creates a safe space for you to take risks." That team was among Google's accomplished groups. By contrast, another engineer told the researchers that his team leader "panics over small issues and keeps trying to grab control." That team did not perform well.

When Google finished reviewing all their data, they found their highest performing teams shared one norm: psychological safety. In these teams, people felt free to share the things that scared them without fear of embarrassment, rejection, or recriminations. They were able to talk honestly about what was messy or sad and have hard conversations with colleagues who were driving them crazy. They didn't have to be focused just on efficiency but could connect with each other in ways that left people feeling heard and valued. They felt safe being vulnerable with each other and learning alongside each other. And they felt able to be themselves.

Why might this be the case? Studies have found that when we treat each other with respect and care it calms our brain's threat system and lights up our reward system. This releases more of the calming hormone oxytocin which makes us more empathetic, trusting, co-operative and forgiving, and reduces our levels of anxiety and stress.

Of course, neither Google or other researchers are suggesting that psychological safety guarantees everything a team tackles will run perfectly or that mistakes will never be made. It doesn't mean team members will never disagree, argue, or feel frustrated with each other. Nor does it ensure team members will never feel uncomfortable or pressured as they hold each other to the highest standards of performance and accountability. Not everyone in a team will be close friends.

But instead of leaking emotional and social energy around these challenges, the presence of psychological safety enables us to focus on having honest discussions, engaging in healthy debates, and sharing accountability. It is what makes it possible for us to be comfortably uncomfortable together as we learn and grow. It can help us to minimize multiple psychosocial risks and more quickly and effectively accomplish our team goals.

> **Mindful Moment:** Are there any key words or phrases you want to add to your "Language Placeholder" to help your team define their goal for psychological safety?

How Psychological Safety Helps Reduce Risk

To understand how psychological safety really impacts our levels of psychosocial risk, we partnered with the Australian Human Resources Institute (AHRI) to survey more than 1,000 randomly selected Australian workers. We found that workers who reported *often* feeling psychologically safe in their team were significantly less likely to be experiencing *any* of the psychosocial hazards listed in Chapter 1. They were also significantly less likely to report feeling burnt out.

Why might this be the case? Because psychological safety facilitates our capacity for candor, vulnerability, and learning together. It helps us feel more confident about requesting improvements to the way our work is organized, to call out a lack of social support when encountered, to address poor working conditions, and to ask for help with bad work experiences as they arise. Instead of biting our tongues in fear, we're more likely to ask for help and seek shared accountability for effective solutions.

Building psychological safety is a "super strategy" when it comes to minimizing psychosocial risk. The data suggests that integrating support for psychological safety within our daily leadership tasks is the smallest and most effective approach to help us identify and navigate the complex and dynamic nature of *all* the psychosocial risks our teams experience.

> **Mindful Moment:** Are there any key words or phrases you want to add to your "Language Placeholder" to help your team understand how psychological safety may help minimize psychosocial risk?

Assessing Psychological Safety

Dr. Amy Edmondson suggests that psychological safety is best viewed as a shared belief that it is safe to take interpersonal risks when working together. Because our beliefs are shaped through a complicated web of social connections, researchers have been exploring how psychological safety is cultivated through a systems lens at the levels of "Me" (individual), "We" (leaders and teams) and "Us" (organization).

For example, studies have found we need to individually learn and practise the skills of perspective taking, inquiry, and compassion that make it easier to share our ideas and concerns ("Me" level). Then we need to practise having conversations within our teams where we can use these skills to integrate multiple perspectives on complex topics and generate novel solutions that are assessed for their effectiveness as we go ("We" level). And, our workplaces need to value, support, and celebrate these behaviours ("Us" level).

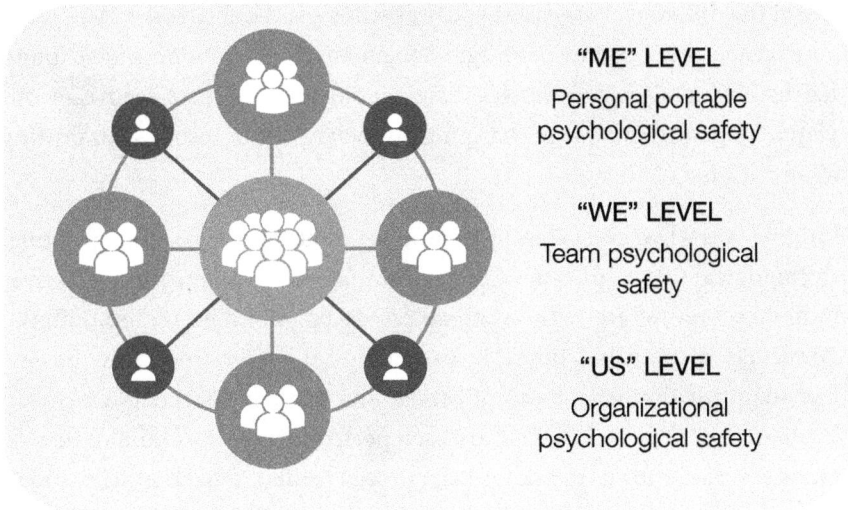

"ME" LEVEL

Personal portable psychological safety

"WE" LEVEL

Team psychological safety

"US" LEVEL

Organizational psychological safety

Figure 4: Me, We, Us Levels

So, how can you assess your current levels of psychological safety and the impact it is having on your ability to minimize psychosocial hazards through a systems lens?

Assessing The "Me" (Individual) Level

Feelings of safety are subjective. What feels safe for one person can feel like a significant risk to another. For example, while a workload that endangers people's lives would feel unreasonable to all of us, speaking up about a continuously high workload with demanding deadlines would feel safe for some of us and completely threatening to others.

Why? Because who we are (i.e., our age, gender, ethnicity, etc.), our experiences of the world, and our perceptions of power, shape what feels safe for each of us in different contexts and with different people. Even though we may be exposed to the same sources or kinds of stress, we often don't respond in the same way because of individual and environmental differences.

One of the differences we can shape is psychological safety at the "Me" level. For example, MIT professors Edgar Schein and Warren Bennis have found that feeling safe inside ourselves is essential for us to feel secure in our relationships and capable of changing our behaviour in response to shifting organizational challenges.

Building on their research, we propose that our levels of "personal psychological safety" also need to be portable; we feel safe within ourselves no matter who we are with, what we are doing, or where we are doing it. Our levels of personal portable psychological safety free us to be less dependent on the behaviours of others and the environments we are in because we understand that we are each perfectly imperfect human beings. It makes it easier for us to ask for help, to seek feedback, to take risks, and to own our mistakes because we believe there is no shame in learning.

For example, while we may feel completely safe with most of our colleagues, there may be one person (or more) with whom we struggle to connect at work. We might feel unsafe with them and blame them for not being "trustworthy". But, perhaps our feelings of discomfort are also a reflection of a lack of trust in ourselves; our inability to speak up and ask for what we need or to set boundaries? Being able to draw on our psychosocial safety in this situation may help us feel safe enough to build the relationship.

Likewise, at work there may be times when the uncertain or uncontrollable nature of what is unfolding leaves us feeling at risk. Typically, we blame our circumstances (i.e., our culture, processes, policies, technology, workspaces, etc.) for failing to provide a safe environment. And while that may indeed be the case, having an increased sense of personal portable psychological safety may help us navigate the difficulties with more confidence. For while we can't change other people and we can't always change our work situations, we can change ourselves and our approach.

Personal portable psychological safety allows us to control the only factor that is ever really within our control – ourselves.

Assessment: Personal Portable Psychological Safety

To assess your levels of personal portable psychological safety, think about your experiences and feelings over the last two weeks at work. Indicate how often you experienced each of the following statements, from 0 = 'Never' through to 10 = 'All the time':

PPPS Factors	Description	Frequency (0 – 10)
Judgment	I was disapproving and judgmental about my own flaws and inadequacies.	
Over-Identification	When I experienced problems, I was consumed by feelings of anxiety and worry.	
Isolation	When I was struggling, I tended to separate and cut myself off from others.	
Help Seeking	I felt it was best to keep my struggles to myself at work.	
Total	**Add the four items together.**	

Scoring:

- If your personal portable psychological safety total is: 0 – 12, it is considered healthy, 13 – 31 is considered moderate, 32 – 40 is considered lower than ideal.

- Your scores for each of the personal portable psychological safety factors are as important as the total score. If your score for any of the items was 3 or below, these are the strengths you can build on. If your score for any of the items was 4 or above, it is worth seeking the knowledge, tools, and support you may need to improve the levels of safety you feel within yourself. And with this in mind, Chapter 5 has an evidence-based toolbox to help you.

Assessing The "We" (Leaders And Teams) Level

There is often a significant gap between the psychosocial support leaders say they are providing, and the hazards team members say they are experiencing. For example, in our research with Australian workers, 92.5 percent of leaders reported they were *often* taking actions to minimize the risk of poor change management for their team, and yet 80.9 percent of team members said they were *often* experiencing this psychosocial hazard. Something about these numbers doesn't add up.

Perhaps, the actions leaders took were not effective or not being prioritized often enough to reduce the risk for their teams. Or, maybe some team members' levels of personal portable psychological safety meant no matter what their leader did, they were more likely to frequently experience the psychosocial hazards. Or, it could be that organizational choices were undermining the efforts of both leaders and workers to build psychological safety and minimize psychosocial risks.

The best way to eliminate this safety gap is to openly discuss your team's experiences so together you can figure out what's working, where people are struggling, what you're all learning, and how you can make the ways you're working together safer for everybody. The challenge of course, is if psychological safety is low in your team, even your most well intentioned conversation is unlikely to yield the insights, learning, or, accountability required to identify and close your safety gaps.

Assessment: Team Psychological Safety

To assess the levels of psychological safety in your team, think about your experiences and feelings over the last two weeks at work*. Indicate how often you experienced each of the following statements from 0 = 'Never' through to 10 = 'All the time':

Psychological Safety Factors	Description	Frequency (0 – 10)
Trust	I felt respected and valued by my team.	
Safety	My team was a safe place to bring up problems and be honest about mistakes.	
Care	My team was encouraging and supportive of one another.	
Total	**Add the three items together.**	

*Ideally, you'd have other members of your team also complete these questions if this feels safe for people to do so.

Scoring:

- If your team psychological safety total is: 0 – 9, it is considered lower than ideal, 10 – 23, is considered moderate, 24 – 30, is considered healthy.

- Your scores for each of the team psychological safety factors are as important as the total score. If your team's score for any of the items was 8 or above, these are the strengths your team can build on. If the score for any of the items was 3 or below, it is worth seeking the knowledge, tools, and support your team may need to improve the levels of safety for these factors. Chapter 6 has an evidence-based toolbox to help you.

Assessing The "Us" (Organization) Level

Dr. Mandy O'Neill's research has found workplaces that prioritize a culture of care positively impact levels of safety, wellbeing, and performance, and offset the impact workplace anxiety has on burnout and organizational costs. Based on Dr. Amy Edmondson's and Mandy's research, we asked Australian workers to rate their workplace cultures along two dimensions – high to low levels of safety and high to low levels of care (see Figure 5).

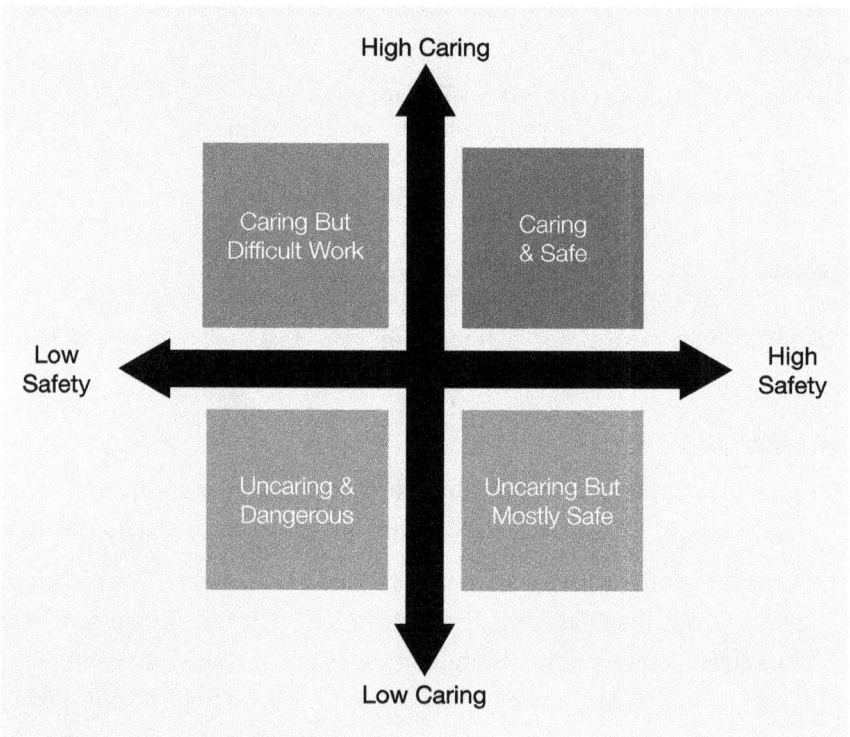

Figure 5: State of Workplace Safety

We found that people working in organizations perceived as "Caring & Safe" reported the highest levels of performance, psychological safety, and wellbeing. They also reported the lowest frequencies of psychosocial risks, particularly for unachievable job demands and inadequate reward and recognition. Those in cultures of "Caring But Difficult Work" had similar, but slightly less favorable results.

By contrast, while those in "Uncaring But Mostly Safe" workplaces did better overall than those in "Uncaring & Dangerous" workplaces, the presence of safety alone failed to reduce the frequency of exposure to the psychosocial risks relating to lack of role clarity, lack of supervisor support, poor workplace relationships, and poor change management.

Why might this be the case? Studies have found that a workers' perceptions of organizational support mediate the mechanism of psychological safety. When people believe their organization respects, values, and appreciates their contributions, and cares about their wellbeing, they report higher levels of psychological safety.

So how can we build workplace cultures of safety and care? Our research found "Caring And Safe" workplaces prioritize the following practices:

- **Compassion** – they create safe spaces for learning and allyship to flourish.

- **Appreciation** – they value strengths and are constantly looking for ways these can be built upon.

- **Responsibility** – they are clear on their commitments to people, planet, and profits and hold themselves accountable.

- **Emotional Wisdom** – they understand the emotional norms, artifacts, and assumptions of an organization impact the bottom line.

Assessment: Workplace CARE Practices

To assess the levels of safety and care in your workplace think about your experiences and feelings over the last two weeks at work*. Indicate how often you experienced each statement from 0 = 'Never' through to 10 = 'All the time': Column headings below?

CARE Practices	Description	Frequency (0 – 10)
Compassion	My workplace had clear policies against bullying and harassment.	
Appreciation	My workplace paid me fairly.	
Responsibility	My workplace cared about my wellbeing as much as it cared about productivity and performance.	
Emotional Wisdom	My workplace had a culture that encouraged inclusivity and belonging.	
Total	**Add the four items together.**	

*Ideally, you'd have other members of your team also complete these questions if this feels safe for people to do so.

Scoring:

- If your workplace care total is: 0 – 12, it is considered lower than ideal, 13 – 31 is considered moderate, 32 – 40 is considered healthy.

- Your scores for each of the workplace CARE factors are as important as the total score. If your workplace score for any of the items was 8 or above, these are your cultural strengths. If the score for any of the items was 3 or below, these are cultural risks that need to be addressed. Chapter 7 has an evidence-based toolbox to help you.

Mindful Moment: Are there any key words or phrases you want to add to your "Language Placeholder" to help your team define safety and care at the "Me", "We", or "Us" level? Are there other existing mental health or wellbeing key words or phrases your team already uses to help them define safety and care?

As powerful as psychological safety is, it can also be fragile. To make it robust and sustainable we need to support the development of internal resources such as personal portable psychological safety ("Me"), and we need to continue investing in our external environment at the team level [SD1] ("We"), and through organizational support ("Us" level).

For leaders, this means we need to understand that rather than grand gestures, psychological safety is built moment by moment as each person – including you – is encouraged to navigate their own fears, as teams give each other permission to stumble, learn, and grow together, and as workplaces enable and sustain healthy ways of working. It requires curiosity, humility, and the commitment to a never-ending series of small steps, regular conversations, and the occasional large leap as the world in which we work continues to change.

The good news is that building psychological safety not only helps our teams to minimize psychosocial risks, it can also help us care for our wellbeing. When we have safe spaces to talk with each other about what's working well, where we're struggling, what we're learning, and how we want to adapt, our data has found workers are more likely to report higher levels of every wellbeing factor.

What The Codes And Legislation Missed

Each of the psychosocial codes and legislation share a version of the same goal – to promote psychological health and wellbeing by preventing harm, intervening early, and supporting recovery. Designed through a risk management lens, the codes and legislation requirements are over-whelmingly focused on eliminating or minimizing risk to protect people's mental health. However, generally they fail to clearly state what the workplaces' responsibilities are for promoting wellbeing.

Does this matter? As Dr. Martin Seligman points out, for more than half a century, psychologists were focused on the study of mental illness and how to fix what erodes wellbeing. While a good deal was learnt about how to ease a range of disorders, very little was discovered about how to support wellbeing. It turned out that relieving the states that make our lives miserable did little to help build the states that make our lives worth living.

We believe the same is true for how we work. While minimizing psychosocial risks and protecting people's mental health should be a basic safety requirement of every workplace, this alone will not be enough to support people's wellbeing. As the World Health Organization notes: "Health is a state of complete physical, mental, and social wellbeing, and not merely the absence of disease or infirmity."

For example, eliminating the risk of unachievable job demands doesn't guarantee we're also being given the opportunity to do meaningful work that engages our strengths, allows us to learn and grow, and leaves us feeling quietly proud and satisfied at the end of a day. And yet, studies have found that opportunities to experience engagement, meaning, accomplishment, and positive emotion are essential to our ability to feel good and function effectively (to be well).

Protecting our mental health and promoting our wellbeing are two different goals that require different measures, strategies, and tools to be accomplished. Unfortunately, the current requirements of the codes and legislation only provide half the solution. And, the danger is that in the rush to comply with their risk management responsibilities, workplaces will neglect the need to invest in wellbeing and will be left wondering why their people struggle to remain engaged, energized, and productive.

We don't want this for you, your team, or your workplace. Because, while our data found that one-in-five Australian workers reported *often* experiencing feelings of burnout and need their workplaces to help protect their mental health, other studies have found that 93 percent of Australian workers say their physical, emotional, and social wellbeing is just as important as the salary they are being paid.

Surely, we need a five-out-of-five person approach to workplace mental health and wellbeing. So, how can you bring together your responsibilities for minimizing psychosocial risks to protect mental health, and your opportunities for building psychological safety, to promote wellbeing (see Figure 6 below)?

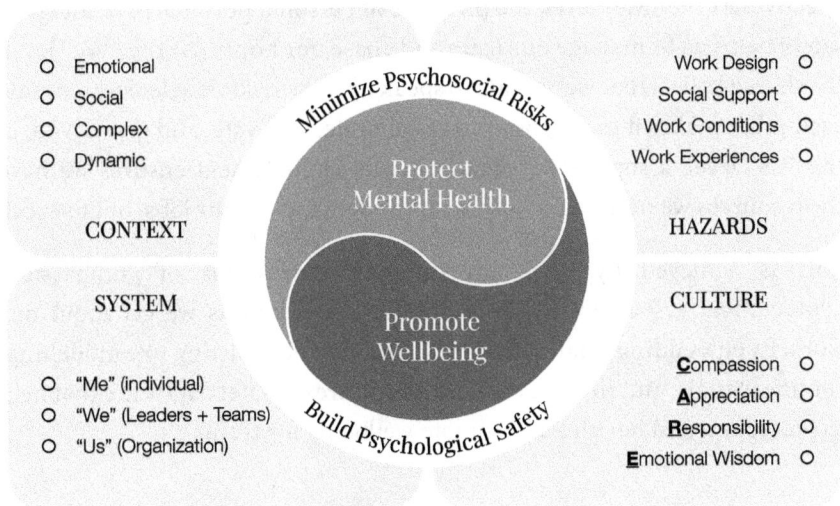

O Emotional	Work Design O
O Social	Social Support O
O Complex	Work Conditions O
O Dynamic	Work Experiences O

Minimize Psychosocial Risks

Protect Mental Health

CONTEXT

HAZARDS

SYSTEM

CULTURE

Promote Wellbeing

O "Me" (individual)	Compassion O
O "We" (Leaders + Teams)	Appreciation O
O "Us" (Organization)	Responsibility O
	Emotional Wisdom O

Build Psychological Safety

Figure 6: Safety & Wellbeing Guide

We need to remember that psychosocial risks are emotional and social, and this creates a context that is complex and dynamic. Our experience of these risks is subjective; what feels safe for us can feel completely unsafe for one of our team members. And, unlike many physical workplace hazards, minimizing or eliminating these risks will never be "won-and-done", but an ongoing day-by-day requirement.

The list of potential psychosocial hazards in most workplaces is long and they tend to appear in groups, rather than as isolated risks. Trying to stay on top of identifying these risks and "controlling" them, as the codes and legislation require, could easily be a full-time job in itself. While tailored actions to minimize or eliminate specific hazards will be required, leaders need ways to integrate these new responsibilities into their existing ways of working.

Building psychological safety at the "Me" (individual), "We" (leaders and teams), and "Us" (organization) level is a "super strategy" that can make navigating psychosocial risks and building wellbeing easier and more effective. At the "Me" level, the presence of personal portable psychological safety helps us to manage our fears and chase our hopes. At the "We" level. the shared beliefs that we are safe to speak up, take risks, and learn alongside each other makes it easier for us to collaborate, innovate, and grow. And, at the "Us" level, a supportive organizational environment ensures we have the resources we need to not just meet the demands of our jobs, but to excel.

This is achieved by *often* investing in expressions of compassion, appreciation, responsibility, and emotional wisdom as we go about our work. By embedding small actions of CARE into our existing role modelling, routine, rituals, and rhythms, we create cultures of safety and care that help to protect mental health and promote wellbeing for teams.

Mindful Moment: Are there any key words or phrases you want to add to your "Language Placeholder" to balance the need to protect mental health and promote wellbeing? Could the Safety & Wellbeing Guide or a similar visual be helpful for your team to understand and remember the approach you are taking together?

How Will You Talk About Safety And Care?

Words and conversations shape our human worlds. They have the power to pull us towards new possibilities that fuel us with hope and neurologically fire up our brains to seek out solutions.

As you look at your "Language Placeholder" take a few minutes to reflect on:

- What's working well? Put an asterix (*) next to the ideas, phrases, or words that are evidence-based, simple, relatable, and memorable.

- Where is the draft language struggling? 'Put an exclamation mark (!) next to the ideas, phrases, or words that aren't evidence-based or don't feel simple, relatable, or memorable.

- Based on your reflections, what are the final words and phrases (maybe even images if your team are visual thinkers) that make it easier for your team to talk with each other about "safety" and "care" at work?

A rough first draft is all you need for now. Then revisit this over the coming days and see what stayed with you and was easy to remember, and what may need adjusting. And when you're ready – without needing it to be perfect – use the tool below to share your "Language Placeholder" with your team. Remember, making it safe for them to speak up, take risks, and learn alongside each other is an essential step towards building more psychological safety.

After all, as Dr. Brené Brown notes: "Language is the greatest tool for meaningful connection. Having access to the right words changes everything."

Team Tips For Building Your Shared Language Guide

We've all experienced moments when a word or a phrase is used that makes no sense to us. It can leave us feeling confused, incompetent, and excluded, unless we feel safe enough to ask someone to explain what was meant and why it matters.

Language is one of the most powerful and affordable tools we have to connect with each other. Spending 60 minutes with your team to co-design your Shared Language Guide for safety and care is likely to be one of the most important ways you can help to minimize psychosocial risks and build psychological safety.

You can lead this conversation with your team or ask a trusted facilitator to hold this space so you can actively participate. Either way, bring your team together, virtually or face-to-face, in a quiet space where people can be present, and everyone's voice can easily be heard.

Once you are all together, we suggest the following steps:

1. **Share What You're Learning About Safety & Care**

   Briefly (10 minutes or less) share what you're learning about the science and practice of building a culture of safety and care, including the importance of language. There is no need to pretend to be an expert, simply share what you're discovering and why you believe this is an important conversation for your team.

2. **Allow People to Reflect**

   Share your "Language Placeholder" and/or our draft or your updated draft of the Shared Language Guide. (We recommend printing these out if you are in a room together or putting them in an online file so people can easily copy and edit.) Allow people 5 – 10 minutes to reflect on:

- What's working well about the draft language? Put an asterix (*) next to the ideas, phrases, or words that are evidence-based, simple, relatable, and memorable.

- Where are we struggling with the draft language? Put an exclamation mark (!) next to the ideas, phrases, or words that aren't evidence-based or don't feel simple, relatable, or memorable.

- Based on your reflections, what 3 changes would you strongly recommend adding, amending, or deleting in the draft language?

3. Invite People to Share

In small groups of 2 – 4 people, so everyone feels safe to speak and all voices are heard, invite people to share their reflections with each other (allow approximately 20 minutes).

- Ask each person to share the three changes they would strongly recommend adding, amending, or deleting in the draft language.

- When everyone has shared, ask each small group to identity the 3 – 5 changes they would most like to add, amend, or delete in the draft language, and to note these down so they are ready to share.

4. Build Your Language Together

- Ask each group to share their recommendations for changes to the draft language. Don't defend. Don't debate. Just listen. Make sure every group is heard.

- Ask if anyone would like to work with you to see how these recommendations can be fused into a final draft for everyone's feedback. Make this a genuine invitation without "voluntelling" or pressuring the group.

- Accept that if no one volunteers, they are happy for you to lead the next step. If people do volunteer, agree to meet as quickly as possible to review all the recommendations and prepare a final draft.

When as many of the recommendations as possible have been incorporated into a final draft, share it back with your team. We recommend this is done as another conversation rather than by email so you can use this opportunity to appreciate and value people's contributions. This can be integrated into an existing meeting or scheduled as a stand-alone conversation.

When you next come together, if other team members have assisted in the drafting, let them lead the way in sharing what has been designed. And be sure to:

- Thank your team for all their input.

- Explain how their feedback has been incorporated into the Language Guide.

- Invite any last reflections or tweaks.

- Celebrate your accomplishment together.

- Ask how they would like to incorporate your Shared Language Guide into the ways you are working together (i.e., posters, screen saver, a language reminder at the start or end of meetings, etc.)

These are just our suggestions based on successful workshops we have run for clients around the world. The steps can be amended in any way that will feel safe and caring for your team.

PART II
INVESTING IN EVALUATION

"The goal is to turn data into information, and information into insight."

Carly Fiorina

Researchers have found the more frequently we experience a sense of progress, the more likely we are to feel intrinsically motivated, optimistic, satisfied, creatively productive, and connected to others at work. But when it comes building a culture of safety and care, experiencing a sense of progress can be challenging due to the complex and dynamic nature of psychosocial hazards. Fortunately, investing in evaluation tools that are safe and trusted can be a powerful way to make people's experiences more visible and actionable.

The best psychosocial evaluation tools should embed your shared language by assessing the beliefs, feelings, and behaviours your team have agreed are important for minimizing psychosocial risks and building psychological safety. In addition, it is essential that the way the tools gather information and insights from your team does not cause more work-related stress. This means using evidence-based approaches to ensure every voice can be equally heard, that people feel safe to speak up, and that the insights people provide are valued and treated with respect.

So, which psychosocial evaluation tool will be best for your team?

We recommend using:

- **Quantitative self-report surveys** – These quick, effective, and confidential tools can gather reliable and actionable evaluation insights from your team or across your entire workplace. Your workplace may already have survey tools that gather psychosocial data along with other information, such as an employee engagement survey. Or you may wish to try a survey tool designed specifically to capture the hazards such as "The PERMAH Wellbeing Survey Tool" or our "Leading With Safety & Care Survey Tool".

  It is important to note that the data gathered through these tools is determined by what people choose to share about themselves; fears about personal confidentiality and fatigue from repeated organizational surveys can compromise the quality of the information collected.

Instead, using trusted third-party tools to gather and store people's de-identified data, providing people with immediate insights they value, and quickly demonstrating the affirmative action being taken based on their feedback, can help overcome these limitations.

So that you can get moving on this aspect of evaluation, we'll share the recommended self-assessment questions from our "Leading With Safety & Care" Tool in Chapter 4.

- **Team conversations** – If you have clear questions, you listen more than you speak, and you reflect on what the emerging patterns and insights might mean in terms of next steps conversations with your team are valuable informal research opportunities. For this approach to be effective, your team needs to feel safe speaking up and know that nothing they say will be used against them. You also need to be mindful and aware of your own biases, so that you hear what your team are really saying and not just what you want to hear. This is difficult for even the most experienced researchers which is why checking what you've heard back with your team or inviting an independent observer of the conversation to do so, can make this information gathering process safer and more reliable for everyone.

So that you can make a start on research conversations with your team, we'll share one of our favorite leader research tools – the "Safety Check Chat" – with you in Chapter 5.

- **Qualitative Research** – Thirdly, having a coach, facilitator, or researcher gather formal feedback from your team, either as a group or through one-on-one conversations, can be an effective means of gathering qualitative data and information. Be sure to be clear and transparent about the purpose of these conversations, who is being asked to participate, and what will be done with the data gathered so that participants can feel confident and safe in their involvement.

Once the feedback conversations are completed, ask the provider you engage to prepare a de-identified report of the findings so that individual confidentiality is protected (unless otherwise agreed) and to help you and your team agree on the actions to be prioritized and taken. This doesn't have to be an expensive or time-consuming exercise. We've used approaches like appreciative inquiry – an action-based research methodology – to safely hold these conversations, debrief the findings, and help leaders and teams agree actions in less than a day, even with hundreds of participants.

Let's start gathering data!

CHAPTER 3

Assessing Psychosocial Safety & Care

In a world of constant change, we are neurologically wired to seek out patterns to help us make accurate predictions that can shape our plans and drive our actions. When we do so, our stress hormones are lowered and a cocktail of feel-good chemicals, including dopamine and serotonin, are triggered in our brains, leaving us feeling more confident and in control. Our brains love the promise of factual data because it provides us with a sense of certainty.

Unfortunately, this desire for certainty often leaves us filling in the data gaps with our biased assumptions and leaping to unfounded judgments. Rather than face the reality that even the best equipped forecasters struggle to accurately predict more than 150 days in advance, we delude ourselves into believing that by basing our plans on factual data we've removed any uncertainty.

Please don't misunderstand. As researchers, we've staked our reputations on gathering and analyzing data in the hope of surfacing actionable insights that can improve the ways we lead ourselves and others. We deeply value the hard work and findings of other thoughtful, credible researchers and believe seeking out evidence-based practices is always the responsible place to start when it comes to the safety and care of our teams.

However, as we noted in the introduction, good science is never proven. Instead, the best researchers are always testing, reviewing, and challenging what we know. Rather than clinging to the illusion of certainty about the "facts", they embrace the limitations as an invitation to keep learning. After all, once upon a time researchers were convinced the world was flat.

Doing No Harm

Studies have found that the most effective leaders let go of their addiction to prediction and prioritize exploration and experimentation by using data and research to:

- **Accelerate their knowledge** – This can be done by gathering data and asking: What's working well and where are they struggling? This makes it easier for them to see and understand the patterns unfolding.

- **Inspire their approaches** – This can be achieved by analyzing the data's actionable insights and other evidence-based ideas. They ask: What are we learning? This helps inform their investments of energy and effort.

- **Experiment and keep learning** – This can be realized by asking: How might we apply what we're learning and adapt, adapt, adapt? This enables leaders to test their chosen approaches, evaluate the impact, and continue adjusting amidst an ever-changing context.

We call this "Running A Research Review".

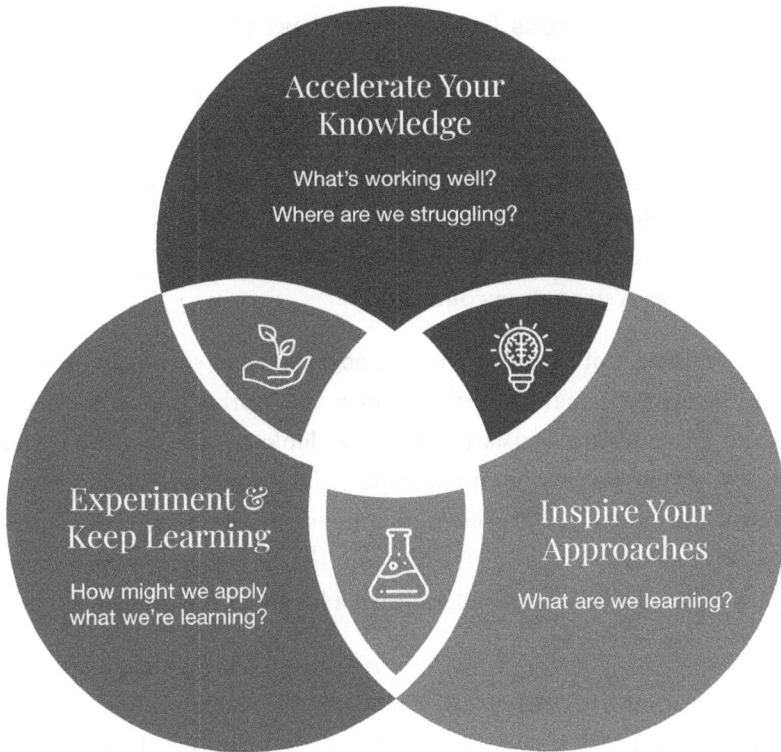

Figure 7: Running A Research Review

The most effective leaders don't do this alone. They invite, empower, and trust their teams to help them find new solutions. And as a result, they resiliently pursue a far richer array of future possibilities as they make the most of the opportunities to safely learn and grow together.

This is what we saw Google do as they sought insights into their highest performing teams in Chapter 2. So, how can we apply this approach ourselves when it comes to assessing the psychosocial safety and care of our teams?

The Need To Assess More Than Just Risks

Just as we recommend that you "Run A Research Review", most psychosocial safety codes or legislation recommend or require workplaces to identify, measure, manage, and monitor the frequency, impact, and duration of risks. Exactly how this data is gathered, analyzed, and acted upon is not specifically stated, but the consultation and inclusion of workers and their representatives is strongly encouraged.

While we agree that assessing the psychosocial risks your team are facing should be a requirement for every leader and workplace, we believe that many of the codes and legislation often overlook the complex and dynamic nature of human behaviour and its impact. For example, while it is essential to assess the individual exposure of your team members to psychosocial risks, without also assessing the support that is being provided and the impact these efforts are having, we learn a lot about the problems but little about the potential solutions.

As Peter Drucker, one of the greatest scholars of leadership and management over the last century noted: "A person can perform only from strengths. One cannot build performance on weakness, let alone on something one cannot do at all." Why might this be the case? Because our strengths represent the ways we are individually and collectively wired to work at our best. They are our patterns of thinking, feeling, and behaving that reflect the things we want to do, we can do, and we will do over and over again.

The challenge is that our brains are wired with a negativity bias that draws our attention towards finding and fixing problems more readily than seeking and building on strengths. When it comes to gathering, analyzing, and actioning data in workplaces, researchers estimate we spend approximately 80 percent of our time focused on what's not working, and only 20 percent of our time looking for ways to build on our strengths. The truth is that neither workplaces, leaders, or teams can excel by simply trying to fixing weaknesses and limiting their failures; it is only by amplifying and magnifying strengths that an upward spiral of learning and growth is created.

Which is why, when it comes to building a culture of safety and care, we recommend assessing psychosocial risks and strengths through a systems lens of "Me", "We" and "Us".

- **"Me" Level – Team Members' Psychosocial Risks:** The frequency with which workers are experiencing the hazards, the impact of these experiences on their wellbeing, and the duration of this impact. This data enables workplaces and leaders to understand which hazards pose the greatest risk to the mental health, wellbeing, and potential burnout of their teams.

- **"We" Level – Leaders' Psychosocial Support:** The frequency with which leaders are trying to minimize or eliminate the psychosocial risks for their team. This data enables workplaces and leaders to understand which hazards they are trying to minimize and what impact their efforts are having. It highlights where safety experience gaps exist between leaders and their team members and gives leaders the confidence to build upon the strengths of their current support efforts.

- **"Us" Level – Workplace CARE Practices:** How often workplaces invest in showing <u>C</u>ompassion, expressing <u>A</u>ppreciation, encouraging <u>R</u>esponsibility, and demonstrating <u>E</u>motional wisdom. This data enables leaders and workplaces to identify the strengths shaping psychological safety and how these can be built upon. It also highlights any capability areas where leaders may benefit from additional training, tools, and support.

Taking a systems lens removes the chance of the data being used to beat leaders into compliance. It avoids the naivety that risks can be eliminated across all teams with a one-size fits all solution. And, it helps to minimize the psychosocial hazard of poor change management by role modelling how a culture of safety and care can be shaped as people solve challenges together.

To help you in your evaluation journey, we've provided the self-assessment tools we use with leaders and teams around the world. These questions have been developed in partnership with other leading researchers based on their published findings and our own large-scale population workplace studies.

You can complete the self-assessments by answering the questions in this book and using the guidance provided to calculate your scores. Or, you can complete our free five-minute Leading Safety & Care Survey Tool which contains the same questions and immediately provides a confidential personal report with all of your results at: **www.theleaderslab.net/survey**.

Completing the assessment tools for yourself can be a helpful first step in considering the safety and care risks and strengths your team may also be experiencing. Given our research has found 68.5 percent of leaders reported feeling burnt out, and that your status and power makes you a highly contagious influence on your team, knowing how you are doing is just as important as knowing how your team are doing. Starting with your own self-assessment will also give you an opportunity to think about the type of questions you may wish to ask your team and how to align the questions towards the shared language you're building.

As you gather your data, we recommend you take a "mindful moment" to pause, reflect, and note your findings, and use the "Running A Research Review" template below to capture what you're learning.

As you review your insights, please remember that people's experiences of safety and care are subjective. This means the frequency, impact, or duration you report may be very different to what your team members are experiencing. The most reliable way to know what is happening is to invite them to complete their own confidential self-assessment tool. We have a paid team option of the Leading Safety & Care Survey Tool available, or you could set up informal or formal team research conversations (see Chapter 4).

As you prepare to answer the questions below it is worth noting that, like all self-report tools, the results will only be useful if the information you provide is as honest and accurate as you can be at this time. This data is just for you, so use the questions below to practice your skills of candor and vulnerability, knowing there isn't a single leader who has psychosocial safety perfectly figured out. At the end of the day, it is your willingness, openness, and ongoing commitment to learning how to be a better leader that will determine your individual and collective success.

Running A Research Review Template

	WHAT'S WORKING WELL?	WHERE ARE WE STRUGGLING?
Psychosocial Hazards		
Leader Hazard Support		
CARE Practices		

WHAT ARE WE LEARNING?	HOW MIGHT WE ADAPT, ADAPT, ADAPT?

"Me" Level: Assessing People's Psychosocial Risks

As noted in Chapter 1, every job involves some psychosocial hazards. When the demands of our work environment exceed our perceived ability to cope with or control them due to deficiencies in the design, organization, and management of work and/or a poor social context, psychosocial risks arise.

Assessment: Psychosocial Risks

Most of us are exposed to a combination of psychosocial hazards as we go about our jobs. Please think about *your* own experiences and feelings over the last two weeks at work:

- In the "Frequency" column, indicate how often you experienced each hazard from 0 = "Never" through to 10 = "All the time";
- In the "Wellbeing" column, indicate the impact of the hazard on your mental health and wellbeing from 0 = "No impact" through to 10 = "Severe impact";
- In the "Duration" column, indicate the duration of the impact of the hazard on your health and wellbeing from 0 = "No time" through to 10 = "Years +".

Hazard / Risk Description	Frequency (0 – 10)	Wellbeing (0 – 10)	Duration (0 – 10)
Work Design			
Lack of role clarity I was unclear about what was expected of me at work.			
Unachievable job demands I was asked to meet unachievable deadlines.			

Hazard / Risk Description	Frequency (0 – 10)	Wellbeing (0 – 10)	Duration (0 – 10)
Low job control I had no choice in deciding how I did my work.			
Inadequate recognition and reward My good work was not recognized and rewarded.			
Social Support			
Lack of supervisor support My direct supervisor did not provide the help and support I needed to do my job well.			
Poor workplace relationships I experienced strained relationships at work.			
Bullying I experienced bullying in my workplace.			
Harassment I was subjected to harassment at work.			
Work Conditions			
Poor change management I was not consulted about changes happening at work.			
Poor physical environment I did not feel physically safe in my work environment.			
Remote work My work required me to spend multiple days away from home.			

Hazard / Risk Description	Frequency (0 – 10)	Wellbeing (0 – 10)	Duration (0 – 10)
Isolated work My work was completed in a location where I was alone.			
Work Experiences			
Poor organizational justice I was not treated fairly by my workplace.			
Violence and aggression I was exposed to violent or aggressive behaviour in my work.			
Traumatic events and materials I was exposed to traumatic events or materials in my work.			

Scoring:

- **Frequency:** 0 – 3, the risk of the hazard is minimized, 4 – 6, the risk of the hazard is moderate, 7 and above, the risk of the hazard is high. Please place an asterix (*) next to the hazards you scored 4 and above on in this column.

- **Impact On Wellbeing:** 0 – 3, the wellbeing impact is low, 4 – 6, the wellbeing impact is considered moderate, 7 and above, the wellbeing impact is high. Please place an exclamation mark (!) next to the hazards you scored 4 and above on in this column.

- **Duration Of Wellbeing Impact:** 0 – 3, the duration of wellbeing impact is low, 4 – 6, the duration of wellbeing impact is moderate, 7 and above, the duration of wellbeing impact is high. Please place a dollar sign ($) next to the hazards you scored 4 and above on in this column.

Any hazards now marked with an asterix (*), exclamation mark (!), and dollar sign ($) currently pose the greatest risk for your mental health and wellbeing. If your workplace and leaders are not already taking action to help you address these risks, it is worth alerting them to what is happening for you. Likewise, any hazards marked with an exclamation mark (!) and/or a dollar sign ($) – particularly if the score is 7 or above – should be immediately addressed.

Mindful Moment: Which psychosocial hazards currently pose the least risk to your wellbeing at work? Which psychosocial hazards currently pose the most frequent and greatest risks for your wellbeing? What might these insights help you learn about psychosocial risks in your team? What adjustments, if any, do they suggest may be worth experimenting with? Note these insights down on your "Research Review".

"We" Level: Assessing Leaders' Psychosocial Support

As we learned in Part I, it is in the interest of every leader to help their team stay safe. To achieve this goal, we need to understand more than just the psychosocial risks people are experiencing; we also need to understand what impact our efforts to support and protect them are having. Only with this data can we identify how to continue building on our current strengths to address future risks.

Assessment: Leaders' Psychosocial Support

Let's begin by helping you to identify how you are supporting and protecting your team from psychosocial risks. Think about *your* own actions over the last two weeks at work:

- In the "Frequency" column, please indicate how often you have taken actions to minimize each hazard from 0 = "Never" through to 10 = "All the time";

- In the 'Impact' column, please indicate the effectiveness of your efforts when it comes to minimizing the hazard from 0 = "None" through to 10 = "Extremely".

Hazards / Actions Taken	Frequency (0 – 10)	Impact (0 – 10)
Work Design		
Lack of role clarity I clearly communicated with my team about what I expected of them.		
Unachievable job demands I ensured my team always had achievable deadlines.		
Low job control I gave my team choices in how they did their work.		

Hazards / Actions Taken	Frequency (0 – 10)	Impact (0 – 10)
Inadequate recognition and reward I recognized and rewarded the good work of my team.		
Social Support		
Lack of supervisor support I provided the supervision and support my team required.		
Poor workplace relationships I helped my team to develop healthy working relationships.		
Bullying I immediately addressed behaviours in my team that might be considered bullying.		
Harassment I immediately addressed behaviours in my team that might be considered harassment.		
Work conditions		
Poor change management I consulted with my team about changes happening in our work.		
Poor physical environment I ensured my team's work environment was physically safe.		
Remote work I acknowledged the challenges experienced by my team members who were away from home for multiple days.		
Isolated work I created opportunities to connect for team members whose work was completed in a location where they were alone.		

Hazards / Actions Taken	Frequency (0 – 10)	Impact (0 – 10)
Work Experiences		
Poor organizational justice I treated people in my team fairly.		
Violence and aggression I minimized the risk of my team's exposure to violent or aggressive behaviour.		
Traumatic events and materials I minimized the risk of my team's exposure to traumatic events and materials in their work.		

Scoring:

- **Remove hazards that are not applicable:** As you consider the support you are providing you may have found that some of your support scores are quite low because the psychosocial hazard poses no risk for your team (i.e., traumatic events). If you believe there are hazards on the list that pose no risk to your team, please exclude them from your "Research Review" for now (check your hazard assessment from Chapter 1 and be sure to review this with your team).

- **Frequency:** If the risk of the hazard needs to be minimized for your team, then a score of 0 – 3 suggests the frequency of your current support is unlikely to have the desired impact, 4 – 6 suggests the frequency of your current support is likely to be having some impact, 7 and above suggests the frequency of your current support is likely to be very impactful. Please place an asterix (*) in the column next to the hazards you scored 7 and above. These are likely to feel as minimized as you can make them for your team.

- **Impact:** If the risk of the hazard needs to be minimized for your team, then a score of 0 – 3 suggests the positive impact of your current support is likely to be low, 4 – 6 suggests the impact of your current support is likely to be moderate, 7 and above suggests the impact of your current support is likely to be high. Please place an exclamation mark (!) in the column next to the hazards you scored 7 and above. These are likely to feel as minimized as you can make them for your team.

- **Next Steps:** For any hazards you haven't put a line through or marked with an asterix (*) or exclamation mark (!), we recommend considering what leadership actions you need to take to keep your team safe. The first step is to gather more data from your team, either through a self-assessment tool or an informal or formal research conversation, so you can understand how their experiences compare to your interpretation.

Please remember that sometimes we find ourselves trapped in a leadership bubble that creates a safety gap between ourselves and our team. While you may believe you are doing everything you can to support your team, it doesn't always mean it is as frequent or effective enough for what your team needs. In addition, the strategic decisions and actions of your workplace, the type of work your people do, and their own levels of psychological safety may mean that even when you are frequently and effectively addressing the psychosocial risks, the danger can persist. This is why we strongly recommend asking your team for feedback about the support you are providing, either through a self-assessment tool or an informal or formal research conversation.

Mindful Moment: Which psychosocial hazards do you believe you are currently minimizing the most effectively? Which psychosocial hazards may need more of your attention and effort to protect your team from harm? What might these insights help you learn about the support strengths you have for minimizing psychosocial risks? What adjustments, if any, do the results suggest it may be worth experimenting with to build on your strengths? Note these insights down on your "Research Review".

"We" & "Us" Level: Assessing Team CARE Practices

In Chapter 2, we found that workers who reported often feeling psychologically safe in their team, were significantly less likely to be experiencing any of the psychosocial risks. And, workers who believed that their organization was "caring and safe" not only reported the lowest frequency of all of the psychosocial risks, they also reported the highest levels of performance and wellbeing. In addition, we explored and assessed the actions your workplace could take to support a culture of safety and care.

While your workplace's commitment to care matters, as a leader you also have a significant impact on your team's culture due to your authority, influence, and regular contact with your team members. Your words and guidance carry more weight than other team members, and you are most often the source of direction.

Assessing the frequency with which you express care for your team can help you identify and understand the strengths you have to build on to improve levels of psychological safety in your team.

Assessment: Leaders' CARE Practices

Think about *your* own actions over the last two weeks at work:

- In the "Frequency" column, please indicate how often you have practiced the CARE behaviours from 0 = "Never" through to 10 = "All the time";

- In the "Impact" column, please indicate the effectiveness of your CARE behaviours from 0 = "None" through to 10 = "Extremely".

CARE Practices	Actions Taken	Frequency (0 – 10)	Impact (0 – 10)
Compassion	I expressed curiosity rather than judgment when people were struggling.		
Appreciation	I gave my team strengths-focused feedback.		
Responsibility	I held my team accountable for their actions.		
Emotional Wisdom	I helped my team to constructively navigate emotions.		

Scoring:

- **Frequency:** 0 – 3, the frequency of your current CARE practices are unlikely to have the desired impact, 4 – 6, the frequency of your current practices are likely to be having some impact, 7 and above, the frequency of your current practices are likely to be very impactful. Please place an asterix (*) in this column next to the CARE practices you scored 7 and above. These are the strengths you have to build upon.

- **Effectiveness:** 0 – 3, the effectiveness of your CARE practices are likely to be low, 4 – 6, the effectiveness of your practices is likely to be moderate, 7 and above, the effectiveness of your practices is likely to be high. Please place an exclamation mark (!) in this column next to the CARE practices you scored 7 and above. These are the strengths you have to build upon.

- **Next Steps:** For the CARE practices with an asterix (*) or exclamation mark (!), what makes it easy for you to invest in these behaviours so often and why are they so effective? For the other CARE practices, are there ways you can use any of your strengths? Or is it worth seeking out the knowledge, tools, and support you may need? Chapter 6 has an evidence-based toolbox to help you.

Please don't forget the risk of finding yourself trapped in that leadership bubble. Be sure to also ask your team for feedback about the CARE you are providing, either through a self-assessment tool or an informal or formal research conversation.

Mindful Moment: Which CARE practices are you currently prioritizing for your team and what impact might they be having on psychological safety? Are there any CARE gaps that may need more of your energy and effort? What are you learning about how you can use your strengths of CARE to support psychological safety in your team? What adjustments, if any, might it be worth experimenting with to build on your strengths? Note these insights down on your "Research Review".

Using Data To Change Behaviours

While we are always fascinated by the latest data we've helped a workplace or leader to gather, numbers alone are not enough to change people's behaviours. It is the sharing of meaningful and actionable insights that are extracted from patterns in the data – ideally as quickly as possible – that can influence the way people think, feel, and act.

The reality is, we are less concerned about any one score from your assessments (which reflect a snapshot of one moment in time) and are far more interested in your "Research Review", and what you are learning and wanting to experiment with as a result of your reflections.

Why? The complex and dynamic nature of psychosocial risks mean they are always changing.

While you may have very low levels of risk today (and if this is the case – congratulations!), it doesn't guarantee the levels will be the same at your next assessment. Just think about how a change in team members, client requirements, a company restructure, or a global pandemic can change your team's experiences overnight. While a great score today can feel momentarily rewarding, more important is your ongoing commitment to keep learning and experimenting about the best ways to build a culture of safety and care for your team as the world around them keeps changing.

This is why "Running A Research Review" is such an important tool every time you measure. Whether you are using our self-assessment questions or other tools, the most valuable findings from your data will always be found in the lessons it offers and the behaviours it changes.

CHAPTER 4

Team Conversations About Safety & Care

Conversations are the oldest and easiest tool we have for sharing information and for supporting individual and collective learning and growth. As systems researcher Dr. Margaret Wheatley shares: "People have always sat in circles and councils to do their best thinking and to develop strong and trusting relationships. Not in mediations, not in negotiations, not in debates or in public meetings, but in simple truthful conversations where each person has a chance to speak, each person feels heard, and each person listens well."

Teams need opportunities to come together and safely share what people are seeing, feeling, and experiencing. These kinds of conversations give us the opportunities we need to speak more openly, honestly, and confidently about our hopes, our fears, our victories, and our struggles. They are also how we make sense of each other's perspectives and build a shared interpretation of events.

The challenge of course is that when we speak up, our conversations are also more likely to surface differences, confusions, and conflicts that can generate paradoxes and heighten the creative tension between our current reality and our hopes. The truth is that real conversations are inherently messy, often awkward, and at times downright uncomfortable.

While it's tempting to avoid the messy parts of conversations, studies have found that teams who can engage each other in healthy conflict are more likely to report improved levels of decision-making, creativity, and performance. Why might this be? Because when psychological safety exists in a team, our diverse perspectives and ideas are less likely to be viewed as obstacles and more readily explored as opportunities for growth.

So, how can you use informal and formal conversations to safely explore the diversity of your team's psychosocial risks and CARE experiences?

Leading Safe Conversations

Workplace codes and legislation recommend – and in some cases, require – the participation of workers (employees *and* contractors) in identifying psychosocial risks in your workplace. While this can be achieved through the quantitative survey tools we explored in Chapter 3, the complex and dynamic nature of psychosocial hazards mean that often the quickest, most affordable, and effective way to identify and minimize risks is through conversations with your team.

The challenge we find is that leaders who have been primarily focused on "managing" their team, tend to talk more than they listen. As a result, levels of psychological safety in their team are often low, and suddenly inviting members to speak up about their experiences of psychosocial risk is often feared as a management trick to expose people who aren't "team players".

The other difficulty is that even leaders who have been primarily focused on "caring" for their team, find it hard to separate themselves from their own biases when listening to other people's experiences. For example, our confirmation bias means we tend to seek out information that confirms our own experiences. Our stereotyping bias causes us to make assumptions about what we are hearing based on our beliefs about people's personal characteristics (i.e., women struggle more with conflict). And, our recency bias means we tend to give more weight to the most recent information we've received and overlook the historical context.

To overcome these obstacles, MIT Professor Edgar Schein suggests that successfully leading psychologically safe conversations with our team requires us to do three things:

- **Less telling** – If we value accomplishing tasks more than building relationships, telling people what is required of them often feels like the fastest way to get the work done. However, this assumes that we alone have all the information, insights, and expertise needed to determine the best course of action. This is rarely the case, especially when navigating something as complex and dynamic as psychosocial risks.

- **More asking** – If we value building safety and care for our team, we need to role model our willingness to be vulnerable enough to admit we don't have all the answers, to be humble enough to ask for help, and to be trusting enough to learn alongside our team. This requires an ongoing attitude of interest and curiosity to help us ask genuinely open-ended questions about our team members' experiences, ideas, and perspectives.

- **A better job of listening** – If we value inclusive and respectful relationships, we need to give others our full attention and to listen with the goal of understanding, rather than rushing to respond with assumptions or judgments. This means slowing down our responses, being mindful of our own biases, and using reflective statements to seek clarification about what others want us to learn from the conversation. Our goal is not necessarily to reach agreement, but to gain a deeper understanding and demonstrate our appreciation for the other person's perspective.

While Edgar's advice is simple and sound, we find that trying to consistently implement these steps initially pushes most leaders well outside their comfort zone. After all, leaders have usually been promoted because of their ability to get technical tasks done, not because of their abilities to ask great questions and listen to their team members. So, how can we learn to tell less, ask more, and listen to learn?

Paige & Michelle's Stories: Unpacking Conversations With Care

As young, hard-working, task obsessed team members, we were both promoted to leadership roles early in our careers – one of us in the United Kingdom and one of us in Australia. A decade later, we found our ongoing task obsession was making our leadership roles unmanageable.

You see, we grew up in workplaces at a time when "command-and-control" leaders such as General Electric's Jack Welch and Microsoft's Bill Gates were the pin-up role models. When it came to giving our teams a clever answer or a clear instruction, we were both brimming with confidence and determination. But when we needed to improve our learning by asking our team members open-ended questions and really listening to their responses, somehow, there was just "never enough time" to have these conversations.

Initially, when we were leading small teams, this wasn't such a problem. If someone didn't follow our instructions, we would sweep in and save the day by fixing their lapse of motivation or the gap in their abilities by doing the work ourselves (while complaining bitterly about how hard it was to find good staff). But, as our teams grew larger and we found ourselves scrambling more frequently to fix the work of multiple people, we couldn't help but wonder if there was something wrong with our leadership approach.

Needing a more effective way to lead, we each began studying the science of human behaviour. When we separately stumbled across the research of Professor David Cooperrider, the mistake we had been making suddenly became very clear. You see, his studies were repeatedly finding that: "Every action people take is preceded by a question."

What? Take a moment and think about how you came to be reading this book. To arrive at this page, you've asked yourself all sorts of questions which may have included: What is this book about? Is reading it worth my time and energy? What might these ideas mean for my team? Are there more tools coming?

Of course, there is every chance you've not been particularly conscious of any of the questions you've been asking – most of us aren't. After all, we live in a world that desires answers, which means most of us rarely pause to consider the preceding questions. David's studies show that this doesn't mean the questions aren't being asked or that our behaviours aren't being shaped by them.

Understanding David's insights was a humbling moment in our development as leaders. It hadn't been our brilliant answers, or our wonderful instructions, that had driven our teams' actions. Instead, it was the questions they were asking themselves about our requests and their own answers that had been motivating their achievements.

Shaken from the delusion that we could "manage" our teams, we came to accept that one of our most important leadership tasks was to use conversations – and in particular the questions we asked and our ability to listen and learn – to guide and support our teams' performance. At first, despite our best intentions, we struggled to let go of our old control patterns. We tended to ask far more leading questions than genuinely open questions. And, even when we were truly curious and wanted our teams' input, we found it hard to resist directing the conversation to achieve our preferred outcome. As you might imagine, these behaviours did little to improve our teams' levels of motivation, safety, or performance.

What we found, like so many researchers before us, is that changing our behaviours is hard.

This is because when we spend years repeating the same patterns of thinking, feeling, and behaving, our brains build up neurological pathways that make performing these activities easier and more effective. Unfortunately, these neural pathways don't get instantly re-routed just because we have an a-ha moment and want to change the pattern. For many leaders, telling less, asking more, and listening to learn are new skills our brains need to repeatedly practice if we are to lead safe team conversations.

If you've been building these conversational skills for a while, your team is likely to already enjoy high levels of psychological safety and feel comfortable speaking up about their psychosocial risks and CARE experiences. If this is the case, we recommend incorporating these topics into your existing informal and formal conversational rituals and routines.

However, if you are still mastering the skills to lead a psychologically safe team conversation, it can be helpful to have an evidence-based framework and a simple set of questions to guide you. This will help create a safe conversational space more easily, and it will free you to be more present so you can really listen and learn from your team members.

Having the tools to build our informal and formal conversational skills quickly improved the wellbeing and performance of ourselves and our teams. We no longer had to "manage" our people to get things done. Instead, by asking questions and listening to learn, we understood our people's levels of motivation and capabilities for completing a task. We were then able to provide the support, appreciation, accountability, and encouragement – the "care" – they needed to succeed.

Our ability to lead safe conversations has been critical as we've begun to navigate the new responsibilities we have for the psychosocial safety of our teams. Quickly identifying and minimizing emerging risks prevents them from growing into big problems – and that's not just our experience. When we sought guidance from Minter Ellison, one of the world's leading employment law firms, on the best ways workplaces and leaders can help address their responsibilities for psychosocial risks, we were told: "Having open and honest conversations about people's day-to-day workplace experiences is the best way to protect a team."

So, what kind of tools might help you to safely lead conversations about your team's psychosocial risks and CARE experiences?

The Safety Check Chat

We get out of bed every day to create simple, evidence-based tools that even the busiest of leaders can use to support wellbeing and performance. We understand that while leaders want to draw on the latest scientific findings, trying to apply the research can be confusing and challenging. And we know that as leaders juggle days packed with emails to answer, forms to fill out, meetings to attend, and what often feels like a never-ending list of other tasks, the idea of fitting in even one more conversation – no matter how good it might be for us and our team – can be overwhelming.

Which is why we've done the work of pulling apart the best studies about how to build psychologically safe spaces for team conversations, interviewed many of the world's leading researchers, and created a "Safety Check Chat" tool that is quick, reliable, and easy for leaders to use. Our clients have found that they can use this tool for informal and formal conversations about psychosocial risks and CARE experiences in their teams.

In either format, the "Safety Check Chat" asks the following questions:

- **What's working well?** – Remember we discovered in Chapter 3 that we learn little about excellence by studying failure, which is why we recommend always starting with this question. Not only will people's answers build your team's sense of understanding, confidence, and appreciation for the strengths of how they are working together, but it will also surface approaches and resources that can be built on when it comes to minimizing psychosocial risks and expressing more CARE. And even if it feels like almost nothing is working well yet, the fact that you are having this conversation together is a step in the right direction.

- **Where are we struggling?** – There is no shame in struggling which is why we recommend always following with this question. Struggle is simply a signal that you're still learning, just like every other leader and team on this planet. By normalizing struggle, you make it safe for your team to speak up and candidly discuss the psychosocial risks and lack of

CARE they are experiencing. And even if it feels like everything is going really well, there is always more to learn as the world around your team keeps changing.

- **What are we learning?** – By making learning together part of your shared goals, and not just the achievement of outcomes, this question makes it safer for your team to be more candid and vulnerable with each other. Because your team's context and needs keep changing, you are never "won-and-done" when it comes to building a culture of safety and care. This means that while your team's day-to-day outcomes absolutely count, in the end it is your ability to mindfully and proactively support your team's mental health and wellbeing that will make their success sustainable.

- **What do we want to try next?** – This invites your team to co-create the solutions safety and care solutions together. This helps you to all be realistic about your context, available resources, and levels of commitment for implementing changes. It also helps you clarify the next steps that will be taken, who will be responsible for what actions, and how you will continue communicating about the changes.

If these questions feel familiar, it is because we also included some of them in the "Research Review" we shared in Chapter 3. In this case however, rather than asking these questions to help you review survey data, you're using them to create a safe space for conversation.

If, as you chat together, the conversation starts to become quite messy, it is important to know that behind every scathing criticism or expression of cynicism lies someone's unexpressed hope. Rather than leaping into defensive mode or cutting the conversation short – provided everyone is speaking respectfully – we recommend slowing the conversation down and asking about the unmet hopes that underlie the frustration or fears that are being shared.

This can often be achieved with simple questions such as: "Based on your concerns, what would success look like for you?" or "Given our history and limitations, how would you most like to see us move forward?" In our experience, our biggest cynics have often become our greatest champions once they have felt truly heard.

When you're ready to wrap up your "Safety Check Chat", we recommend:

- **Taking accountability** – Role model and clearly communicate the actions you will be taking as the leader to help minimize any identified risks or invest in opportunities for CARE. Share how you will report back on your progress.

- **Inviting participation** – If appropriate, extend a genuine invitation for any of your team to work with you in co-designing the solutions. Please note, people who don't volunteer cannot later be punished. If nobody offers to assist, then simply leave the invitation open in case anyone changes their mind.

- **Expressing appreciation** – Be sure to thank your team for their candor, vulnerability, and willingness to keep learning together. Share your ongoing commitment to build a culture of safety and care and let them know you are always open to their feedback, insights, and ideas.

Be in no doubt that this seemingly simple conversation has the capacity to significantly improve your team's levels of psychological safety, help you quickly find ways to minimize psychosocial risks, and leave your team feeling cared about and cared for. It will be worth every minute of investment.

The Safety Check Chat Poster

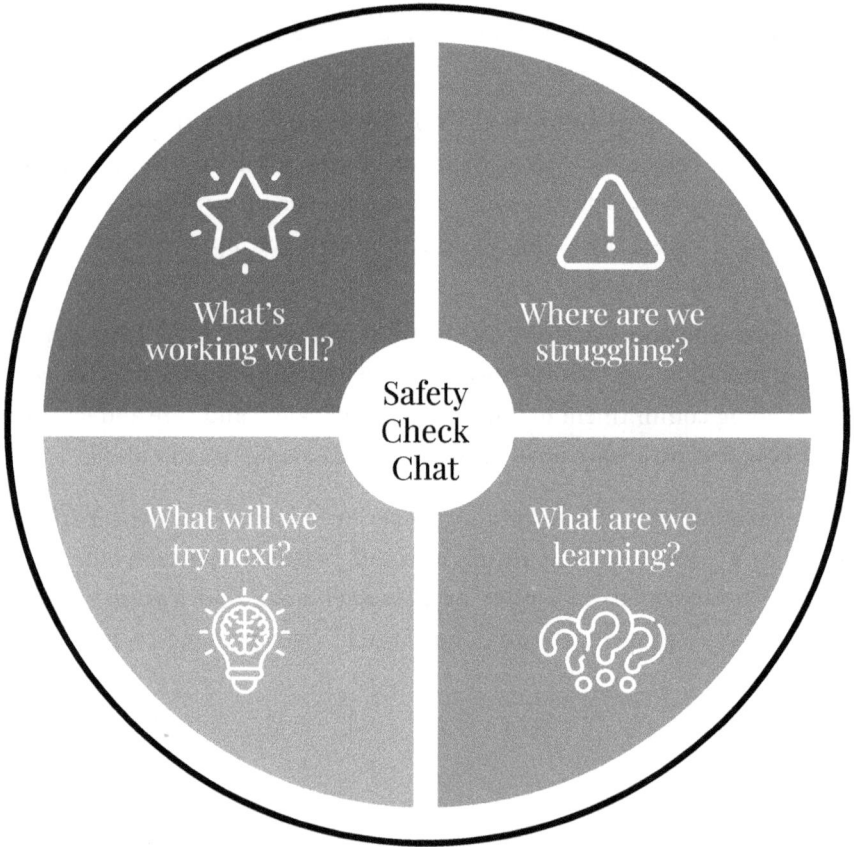

The Safety Summit

Used in thousands of organizations by millions of people around the world, appreciative inquiry is an action-based research methodology that creates psychologically safe spaces for people to navigate complex changes together. Created by Professor David Cooperrider – who taught us about the power of questions – and his colleagues, it can be used for one-on-one, small groups, or entire workplace conversations.

Appreciative inquiry is designed to ensure every voice in a team is equally and respectfully heard and valued (regardless of titles). People come together to explore a series of generative questions that make it safe to see old things in new ways. It uses a variety of conversational tools to make speaking up easier, even when opinions differ dramatically. It draws on design thinking tools to help teams find not just common ground but higher ground as they explore the conversation together. In fact, studies suggest that many people come away from these conversations feeling safer with each other, and more engaged, energized, and ready to help each other make meaningful changes.

For example, we've used appreciative inquiry to help teams have conversations that enable them to:

- **Discover** the strengths and struggles they are facing when it comes to their psychosocial safety and CARE experiences;

- **Dream** of practical ways to build on their team's strengths to help minimize psychosocial risks and express CARE more effectively and frequently;

- **Design** and prototype more effective ways of working that protect mental health and promote wellbeing in their team;

- **Deploy** these ideas by self-organizing around their preferred changes in ways that help them to continue learning and growing together.

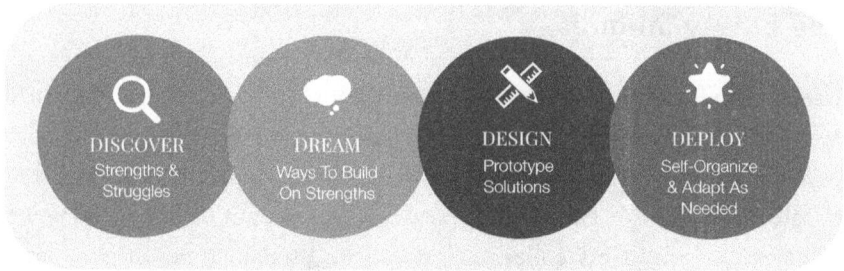

Figure 8: The Appreciative Inquiry Conversation

The duration of these conversations depends on the number of people participating and the depth and breadth of the conversation. For example, a conversation with a single team member may only need 10 to 60 minutes, however a conversation with a small group may need a few hours or a day, and a conversation with hundreds or even thousands of voices is typically held over one to three days.

You can use the example of a Safety Summit Guide below to guide your team through an appreciative inquiry conversation to identify and minimize psychosocial safety risks. Designed for a team of up to 24 people, this conversation should take approximately four hours (you can expand any of the suggested times as you desire, but we do not recommend trying to reduce the times further). If you're doing this as one long conversation, be sure to give people a body break along the way. Alternatively, you can break it up into shorter conversations with one session for discover, one session for dream, and one session for design and deploy. Or, you may choose to stop after discover or dream if that is all the information you need from your team.

Whatever your decision, it is worth considering if it would be beneficial to ask a facilitator, coach, researcher, or peer to lead the conversation for you. This enables you to join your team as an equal participant and demonstrate that your voice is no more or less important than anyone else's. And, if you are concerned about your team feeling safe to speak up in front of you, it also allows you to remove yourself for parts of the conversation.

A Safety Summit Guide Example

Building A Culture Of Safety & Care

Every job involves some psychosocial hazards. The way our work is designed, the social support available, our work conditions, and our work experiences can increase the risk of work-related stress and harm to people's health. These are called psychosocial (emotional and social) risks.

Minimizing these risks and maximizing our experiences of care as we work together is in everybody's best interest. To help us do this today, we're going to discover our current strengths and struggles, dream of what success looks like, design better ways of working, and deploy the actions we most want prioritized.

Throughout this conversation we will ensure every voice is heard, respected, and valued, regardless of job titles. We encourage you to speak up, ask additional questions, and offer ideas, knowing this is a safe space in which no one will be made fun of, rejected, or punished for sharing their experiences or hopes. Our only goal today is to learn how we can better keep each other safe.

[Note: We recommend including in the guide, or having on the tables, the psychosocial hazards poster in Chapter 2 or any updates of your own language around the hazards to help people understand the kind of psychosocial risks they may be experiencing.]

Discover | Sharing Our Tales Of Strength

Activity 1: Paired Interviews (20 minutes)

Find a partner you don't know well and ask them the questions below. You have ten minutes each.

Be sure to take good notes so you can share your partner's stories in the next activity. At the end of your conversation, ask your partner if there is anything they have told you that they don't want you to share in the next activity.

Part A. What are the strengths of care we can build on?

1. Can you tell me about time when you felt respected, supported, and valued in our workplace, in ways that made your job less stressful? It may have been a big thing or a small thing, a regular thing or a one-off, or a recent thing or something that happened a while ago.

2. What made this feeling of being respected, supported, and valued possible? Who was involved? How did it happen? Why did it make your work less stressful? What made it so memorable for you?

Part B. What are the psychosocial struggles we need to learn from?

1. Looking at the list of psychosocial hazards in our workplace, can you share which ones – if any – have been causing you the greatest levels of stress over the past month?

2. Of the hazards you identified, which ones – if any – have you been experiencing frequently? Using a scale of 0 (not at all) to 10 (severe), what impact has this been having on your wellbeing?

Activity 2: Small Group Review (30 minutes)

Join with one or two other pairs to create a group of four or six people. To ensure everyone's voices are heard, please start by asking for volunteers to help: a) lead the discussion; b) keep time; and c) record your team's notes so you can share what you learn.

1. Please take turns introducing your partner and sharing what you learned about their experience of strengths and struggles in the workplace (Part A).

2. You have three minutes each to share. Be sure to listen respectfully to each other so you can try and identify the common strengths and risks in your stories.

3. When everyone has shared, you have ten minutes to work together to:

    *   Identify the five most common causes of success across your stories of care (Part A). Recorder, please note these down under the heading "Strengths".

    *   Identify the biggest psychosocial risks (those happening frequently and having significant impact on wellbeing) that people heard their partners share (Part B). Recorder, please note these down under the heading "Risks".

    *   Finish this sentence based on what you learned: "When it comes to minimizing our psychosocial risks and maximizing our experiences of care, as a team we need to …" Recorder, please note this sentence down.

[Note: We recommend providing sticky notes, large paper, Google Forms, or any other format your people like to use to gather and share their notes. It is helpful if they can see what each group has recorded for the dream activities.]

Activity 3: Large Group Debrief (15 minutes)

Return to our large group. Let's ensure each group's findings are heard.

1. Recorders, please share your group's five common causes of successful care, the biggest psychosocial risks (those happening frequently and having significant impact on wellbeing), and your sentence ending. You have three minutes each.

2. Please be sure to listen respectfully to each group and take notes of the insights that resonate most with you to help you in the dream activity.

3. If time allows, shares any stories of strength or struggle you heard from a teammate, that you feel is important for everyone to hear as we wrap up our discoveries.

Dream | Sharing Our Goals

Activity 1: Small Group Reflection (20 minutes)

Please return to your small group. To ensure everyone's voices are heard, please start by asking for new volunteers to help: a) lead the discussion; b) keep time; and c) record your team's notes so you can share what you learn.

1. Reflect on your individual responses to the following questions. You have five minutes.

    Imagine we have time travelled six months into the future and come together to celebrate our progress on building a culture of safety and care. Based on what we have just discovered about our biggest psychosocial risks and our strengths of care, and being realistic about the time frame and resources available to us:

    *   What were **the small actions** our workplace, leaders, or team had taken that were having a big impact?

    *   What were **the most surprising actions** our workplace, leaders, or team had taken that were making a positive difference?

    *   What were **the bravest actions** our workplace, leaders, or team had taken that made us grateful to be part of this organization?

    Don't overthink your answers. Let them flow. Try to be as specific as you can.

2. Quickly have each person in your group share their hopes for the small actions, the most surprising actions, and the bravest actions. You have ten minutes to make sure you hear everyone, so timer please help your group stay on track.

    Recorder, please capture everyone's ideas under the headings "Small Actions", "Surprising Actions", and "Bravest Actions". If you can, try and group similar hopes together.

    [Note: We recommend providing sticky notes, large paper, Google forms or any other format your people like to use to gather and share their notes. It is helpful if they can see what each group has recorded for the dream activities.]

Activity 2: Small Group Visualization (20 minutes)

Please stay in your small group and keep your volunteer roles.

1. Look at the hopes your recorder has captured. Together, please note what are the great ideas in here you want to try and build on? Ask your recorder to circle these.

2. Work together to create a story that conveys your hopes for minimizing psychosocial risks and building on your strengths of care, using the following Pixar story framework. Recorder, please capture the story and be ready to share:

   Once upon a time _____.

   Every day, _____.

   One day _____.

   Because of that, _____.

   Because of that, _____.

   Until finally _____.

(Example: **Once upon a time** there was a widowed fish named Marlin who was extremely protective of his only son, Nemo. **Every day,** Marlin warned Nemo of the ocean's dangers and implored him not to swim far away. **One day,** in an act of defiance, Nemo ignored his father's warnings and swam into the open water. **Because of that,** he was captured by a diver and ended up as a pet in the fish tank of a dentist in Sydney. **Because of that,** Marlin set off on a journey to recover Nemo and enlisted the help of other sea creatures along the way. **Until finally** Marlin and Nemo found each other, reunited and learned that love depends on trust.)

Activity 3: Large Group Debrief (20 minutes)

Return to our large group. Let's ensure each group's hopes are heard.

1. Recorders, please share your group's story of hope. You have three minutes each.

2. Please be sure to listen respectfully to each group and take notes of the hopes that resonate most with you to help in the design activity.

3. What were the common themes you heard for minimizing psychosocial risks and building on our strengths of care? Were there any big ideas to which you wanted to shout: "Yes!"?

Activity 1: Large Group Exploration Of How Might We? (10 minutes)

As one large group. Let's explore how we can turn our shared hopes into reality.

1. What are the "How might we?" questions you most want us to focus on answering to realize our shared hopes? For example, "How might we better assign work to reduce the risk of unachievable work demands?"

2. As each "How might we?" question is called out, please put your hand up to volunteer if you would like to help co-design a possible solution for this challenge. This will be your group for the next activity.

3. When your "How might we?" group comes together, if you have more than six people, please break into smaller groups to work on the same "How might we?" question so everyone's voices are heard.

Activity 2: Small Group Brainstorm (20 minutes)

In your new small group, to ensure everyone's voices are heard, please start by asking for volunteers to help: a) lead the discussion; b) keep time; and c) record your team's notes so you can share what you learn.

1. Brainstorm solutions to your "How might we question?". Recorder, be sure to capture these ideas. If you can, try and group similar ideas together. Discussion leader, please make sure everyone has a chance to contribute. You have 15 minutes.

2. As a group, select one of your best and most practical ideas to rapidly prototype. If you have trouble narrowing it down, your group can split into smaller teams to work on different ideas. You have five minutes to select the ideas you'd like to prototype today (you can always come back and do more later).

Activity 3: Small Group Rapid Prototype (15 minutes)

In your small group, work together to think about your chosen "How might we?" question and brainstorm ideas to prepare a written Shark Tank style pitch for your prototype that can be shared with the rest of your team. Please use the questions below to guide you:

1. What is the name of your idea?

2. What psychosocial risk/s does your idea help to minimize or how does it build on our strengths of care?

3. How does your idea work practically (try to explain it clearly, step by step, like the instructions for a recipe)?

4. Why are you excited about this idea? What positive difference would it make to our team's ways of working?

5. What would your idea cost?

6. If you'd like to add any visuals or models to demonstrate your idea in action, please feel free to do so.

7. Prepare a two-minute presentation to share your prototype.

Destiny | Support Self-Organization

Activity 1: Large Group Debrief (30 minutes)

Return to our large group. Let's ensure each group's designs are shared.

1. Please present your group's prototype to help minimize psychosocial risks and build on our strengths of care. Each group has two minutes.

2. Please be sure to listen respectfully and jot down any notes of appreciative feedback. What did you really like about their idea? Are there any thoughts you have for making their idea even better? Do you have any information that they need to make their idea successful?

3. If time allows, after each idea is presented, share any appreciative feedback for the group. If time is short, please note your feedback on sticky notes and pass them to the group.

4. When everyone has presented, reflect together on:

   - What are the next steps that you'd prioritize as a team?

   - Who would like to be involved – if anyone – in helping take these next steps? It is okay if no one volunteers. If this is where the energy is in the group for these changes currently, it is better to know that now than wonder why no one is following through later. Talk about this honestly with each other and what it means for how you want to work together as a team.

   - How do you want to progress on the next steps to be shared back to the group? How often would you like to be updated?

Embracing The Conversational Mess

Regardless of which tools you choose, or who leads the discussion, we recommend you prepare to lead safe conversations by carefully considering:

- **The Physical Space** – Where will this conversation be held? Is it a place where people can talk freely, without fear of being overheard or interrupted? If you are coming together in person, be sure to seek neutral ground (i.e., not your office) and somewhere where your team can easily sit together without big table spaces between you. If you are coming together virtually, be sure to choose a platform that people are comfortable using so the technology doesn't present a distraction during the conversation.

- **The Relational Space** – How will you explain why you want to bring your team together for this conversation? How can you put them at ease about your intentions and goals for the conversation? Remember, our brains don't like uncertainty so the more reassuring clarity you can provide in the lead up to the conversation, the safer people are likely to feel when you meet. Then, as the conversation begins, re-state your intentions and be clear that regardless of their job titles, gender, age, nationality, or any other differences, their experiences and ideas will be valued in the discussion.

- **The Conversational Space** – How will you role model listening to learn for your team throughout the conversation? How will you avoid dominating the discussion or becoming defensive? Researchers have found that instead of seeking to control the outcomes, the most successful leaders influence others by talking in ways that signal vulnerability, revealing their own weaknesses, asking for insights and suggestions, and welcoming the co-creation of solutions to deliver win-win outcomes.

Finally, be mindful that even the most carefully planned conversation is unlikely to move in a straight line. Remember that while the differences, confusions, and conflicts that can arise in our conversations often feel uncomfortable and awkward at the time, respectful disagreements have been found to improve a team's learning, creativity, and performance. They are also the skills your team needs to practice with each other in order to build psychological safety.

PART III
SPARKING ACTIVATION

"There is no one magic strategy that will help every person be well."

Sonja Lyubomirsky

With the increasing focus on the science of wellbeing in recent decades, there is a growing toolbox of evidence-based activities that leaders, teams, and workplaces can choose from when it comes to supporting their chosen safety and care outcomes. But which ones will work best for to address the insights you've gathered about your team?

Studies have found the activities likely to be most effective for your team will depend on the psychosocial risks you need to minimize, the strengths of care you have available to build upon, and the ways you work together to achieve your goals. To help make your choices easier, the following chapters contain the most effective tools we've seen applied over the last decade at the "Me" (individual), "We" (leaders and teams) and, "Us" (workplace) levels.

In gathering these tools for you, we were tempted to organize them by applying the compliance mindset with which the codes and regulations have been written to mitigate psychosocial risks. However, as we saw in the research in Chapter 2, minimizing these risks is not the same as building a culture of safety and care.

As we explore the toolboxes in the following chapters, it is important to be clear on your leadership goal with your team. Are you willing to settle for compliance with the psychosocial safety codes and regulations? Or do you want to foster and sustain your team's commitment to working together in ways that support higher levels of wellbeing and performance?

We recommend the latter. Not only will it require less energy and effort in the long-term, it will deliver better returns and leave you feeling proud of your leadership legacy. As Peter Drucker noted: "The task of leadership is to create an alignment of strengths in ways that make a system's weaknesses irrelevant."

With this goal in mind, we have organized the following chapters by applying a strengths mindset for each of the CARE (Compassion, Appreciation, Responsibility, Emotional Wisdom) factors. As you explore the toolboxes, we recommend reviewing your *Evaluation* insights from Part II to:

- **Identify the CARE practices that are already working well in your team.** How might you continue building on these to minimize any psychosocial risks your team are experiencing? How might you use these to improve the frequency and effectiveness of the leadership support you're providing? Remember, you will experience a quicker return on your investments in these CARE practices as you reflect on the ways your team and workplace are already wired to work at their best. These are the tools you want to prioritize.

- **Identify the CARE practices where there is struggle in your team.** Would addressing these gaps help to minimize any psychosocial risks your team are experiencing? How might being more mindful of these gaps shape the leadership support you're providing? These CARE factors will require more energy, effort, and commitment to address, but if you believe they present risks that cannot be minimized in any other way, then please prioritize them.

How To Navigate The CARE Toolboxes

Based on your reflections, note your CARE practice priorities on the "CARE Toolbox" we've provided below and then add a number next to "Priority #". This will help you focus on the CARE tools you most want to experiment with, based on what you have learned about your team.

When it comes to selecting the tools themselves, we recommend compiling a short-list of tools you can share with your team and allowing them to choose what feels meaningful, achievable, and can be easily nudged into your existing ways of working together. Why might this approach be more effective than simply telling your team what you want them to do?

Professors Edward Deci and Richard Ryan have found, over more than thirty years of research, that a sense of autonomy – the opportunity to choose our own actions – has a powerful effect on our levels of motivation, wellbeing, and performance. Rather than feeling coerced to comply, when we're given the freedom to choose activities that are aligned with our personal interests and values, we're more likely to willingly engage our talents, abilities, and energies in ways that leave us feeling energized and satisfied. Far from making us selfish, their studies have found that when people are given autonomy, they are more committed to making choices that are good for everybody.

To help you gather a short-list of evidence-based tools your team can choose from, we recommend reading the first section of each chapter to give you a good understanding of what psychological safety looks like at the "Me", "We", and "Us" levels in your workplace. Then, you may wish to read through all the tools or simply pick the CARE practices that are most important for your current needs.

We have also provided space on your CARE Toolbox to note the psychosocial hazards that each of the CARE practices may help your team to minimize.

Please note, these observations are based on our experiences as there is currently limited research measuring effective interventions to minimize each of the psychosocial hazards. For this reason, we recommend experimenting with any of the tools you think may be helpful for your team and adding to our suggestions.

CARE Toolbox

		TOOL 1		
		NAME	HAZARD	4RS?
Showing Compassion	Me			
	We			
	Us			
Expressing Appreciation	Me			
	We			
	Us			
Encouraging Responsibility	Me			
	We			
	Us			
Demonstrating Emotional Wisdom	Me			
	We			
	Us			

TOOL 2			TOOL 3		
ME	HAZARD	4RS?	NAME	HAZARD	4RS?

CHAPTER 5

Building Psychological Safety At The "Me" Level

Bumping up against our limitations, falling short of our ideals, dealing with setbacks, and owning our mistakes or failures – in other words "learning" – can feel extremely stressful, especially at work. After all, how will anyone respect us, value us, trust us, or like us if they really know just how imperfect we are?

To try and help us feel socially safe, researchers have found our brains can fluctuate between self-serving distortions and ruthless self-criticism. Unfortunately, neither of these strategies make it easy to give ourselves the permission or the support we need to learn and grow at work.

For example, studies have found that many of us think we're funnier, more logical, more popular, better looking, nicer, more trustworthy, more modest, wiser, and more intelligent than others. We even tend to believe that we're above average when it comes to our ability to view ourselves objectively. Of course, logically these numbers just don't add up.

In addition to over-estimating our own abilities, we often significantly under-estimate other people's abilities as we choose to focus most of our attention on their flaws and shortcomings. Why? Because when we see others in a negative light, we feel superior, and believe we are safer in contrast.

Understandably, if we're invested in puffing ourselves up and pulling others down, being confronted with our own imperfections as we learn new skills can come as an unwelcome shock. Fearing we'll be humiliated, excluded, or rejected by others, we often respond by being overly critical and cruelly judgmental of ourselves. Unfortunately, although designed to motivate us towards self-improvement, all these responses really teach us is that failure should be avoided at all costs.

The truth is that while self-aggrandizing and self-judgmental behaviours may initially provide us with a feeling of safety, over time they leave us riddled with insecurities and haunted by the fear that eventually others will discover we're "not good enough", "not smart enough", and "not likable enough". As a result, the slightest threat to our self-concept can quickly trigger our brain's threat-defense responses, causing us to fight ourselves (more self-criticism), flee from others (isolation), or freeze (ruminate and over-identify).

The more we berate ourselves, withdraw from others, or stew in self-doubt, the more vulnerable we feel. And instead of building the beliefs and skills we need to navigate different people and situations safely, we find ourselves caught up in a confusing and painful cycle of mistrust.

So, how can we teach our brains to build the kind of beliefs and skills that make it safe for us to learn and grow alongside others?

How Personal Portable Psychological Safety Makes Learning Easier

Closely aligned with Dr. Kristen Neff's research on self-compassion, building personal portable psychological safety depends on us having the knowledge, tools, support, and emotional wisdom to practice:

- **Relinquishing self-judgment** – Instead of berating ourselves about what failures we are, we invest in comforting ourselves as we acknowledge that we are not where we want to be yet, and encourage ourselves to keep trying. We extend compassion towards ourselves.

- **Rejecting isolation** – Instead of hiding ourselves away so others can't witness our humiliation and unworthiness, we feel brave enough to own our mistakes. We are willing to be vulnerable enough to ask for help and support because we know that every single one of us is failing some of the time. We take responsibility for ourselves.

- **Resisting over-identification** – Instead of feeling helpless and overwhelmed, we reach for openness and curiosity about what is unfolding so we can take a more balanced perspective that enables us to keep learning and growing. We show appreciation for our strengths and look for ways we can build on them.

In other words, we express CARE for ourselves.

Studies have found these self-soothing behaviours activate our brain's caregiving and self-awareness systems, making it easier for us to believe we're capable and worthy, and making us less self-conscious, less likely to compare ourselves to others, and less likely to feel insecure. They have been found to be an effective means of enhancing our motivation, performance, and resilience so we can make informed choices about when it is safe to persist, when we need to try a different path, and when to let go.

DESIRED INDIVIDUAL OUTCOMES	WHEN PERSONAL PORTABLE PSYCHOLOGICAL SAFETY EXISTS	WHEN PERSONAL PORTABLE PSYCHOLOGICAL SAFETY IS ABSENT
Self-compassion is shown to enable belonging and inclusion.	We accept we are still learning, just like every other person in our workplace, and are brave enough to ask for help and support from others.	We believe some people in our workplace know it all and feel ashamed we are still figuring things out, which causes us to isolate ourselves from others.
Appreciation of strengths is expressed to fuel confidence, engagement, and innovation.	We focus on finding ways to build on our strengths – the things we are good at and enjoy doing – and contribute them in meaningful ways towards shared goals.	We focus on appearing perfect and prefer to be always in control of our tasks so no one can discover our weaknesses or flaws.
Responsibility is encouraged to support candor, learning, and growth.	When we are faced with setbacks, mistakes, or failures, we acknowledge we are not where we want to be yet, and own what we need to learn.	When things don't go to plan, we blame other people or circumstances, and are reluctant to consider what is ours to learn.
Emotional wisdom is demonstrated so we can trust and respect ourselves.	We are open and curious about our emotional triggers, and how to navigate the impact our feelings have on our work and relationships.	We are unaware of our emotional triggers and how to navigate the impact our feelings have on our work and relationships.

Figure 9: Personal Portable Psychological Safety Continuum

Your "Me" Level Leadership Challenge

Given the actions and emotions of leaders have been found to be contagious, your levels of personal portable psychological safety can impact your team's levels of psychological safety. For example, researchers have long known that panic spreads, but studies have more recently found that leaders who have low levels of personal safety can have a contagious impact on their team members – particularly those who are also low in personal safety – and influence their thoughts and actions.

If you've ever worked for a leader who relentlessly expected perfection, you've probably experienced how their fear of failure creates a ripple of distrust, spotty implementation, and an inability to learn together. This in turn results in higher levels of anxiety and burnout across a team. This is because when team members feel insecure, they're more likely to automatically mimic their leader's facial expressions, body language, and tone of voice in an effort to build connection. This triggers a variety of physiological and neurological processes that causes them to 'catch' their leader's anxiety, and then act on it.

This can create a cycle of dysfunctional behaviours, group conflict, and impaired decision-making that undermines the feelings of safety for leaders and team members. While studies have found that both negative and positive emotions are contagious between leaders and their teams, more recent research suggests this may depend on your ability as a leader to transmit emotions to others, on your team members' susceptibility to contagion, on shared personality attributes, and the tasks being undertaken.

As leaders, we have a responsibility to ourselves and our team members to ensure we have access to the knowledge, tools, and support we need to care for our own levels of personal portable psychological safety. The toolbox on the following pages of this chapter will give you a good place to start.

We also recommend you seek ongoing conversations with coaches, mentors, and peers. This will provide you with safe spaces for the accountability, feedback, and encouragement it takes to sustain and evolve these skills as the complex and dynamic psychosocial risks your team experiences keep changing.

Your "Me" Level Team Challenge

Much like caring for our wellbeing, at the end of the day navigating feelings of personal portable psychological safety is each person's individual responsibility. While the emotional contagion of others may influence how team members feel, how they choose to think, feel, and act is an inside job. So, what does this mean practically for helping your team to build their own levels of personal portable psychological safety?

As leaders, in addition to your own personal work, you also need to make sure you're giving your team members the knowledge, tools, and support they need to care for their own levels of psychological safety. Be sure to share your CARE Toolbox suggestions, request training for your team members, and, if people need additional support, utilize the coaching, employee assistance programs, mentoring, and peer support programs that exist in your workplace.

Michelle's Story: A Work In Progress

I felt the blood rush from my head and the pain and fear pierce my heart. How could someone I'd given so much emotional, intellectual, and financial support to for three years be accusing me of being greedy and selfish? I'd always felt so safe working with Olivia, but this one horrible exchange smashed apart all the hard-won trust in our relationship. And, my response made me completely doubt myself and my ability to lead others.

Our small team had been navigating a lot of challenges during the preceding years. A growing business needing diverse new team members, a global pandemic requiring constant service pivots, and unpredictable community lock-downs had taken a toll on everyone's resilience levels. There was no denying the culture of our team and our ways of working had changed significantly, but our commitment to building our individual and collective levels of psychological safety meant that we had been able to navigate these changes well together.

When changes had to be made, we communicated clearly and transparently. When team members clashed, we supported ownership and accountability to find better ways forward together. When we heard team members talking about their frustrations with others, we consistently encouraged them to talk to each other as they learned how to each play to their strengths. No question was too silly, no idea too dumb, and no mistake too catastrophic that we weren't committed to safely learning from as a team.

As a leader I prided myself on role modelling how to care for my personal portable psychological safety. I had learned how to:

- Recognize feelings of anxiety and fear as simply my body's way of letting me know that something important to me was unfolding and needed my attention. Daily emotional wisdom practices meant it was increasingly rare for these uncomfortable emotions to hijack how I responded to people or situations.

- Let go of self-judgment and keep my inner critic on a short leash when things weren't going the way I wanted. Lots of self-compassion practice had taught me I wasn't a "loser" who could never get things right, I was just someone who was still learning and hadn't mastered the skills I needed, yet.

- Reject my desire to hide away when I felt embarrassed or ashamed about mistakes I'd made or people I'd let down. Plenty of taking responsibility practice had helped me learn that the more quickly I took accountability, and was willing to be vulnerable enough to ask for help, the faster these painful moments passed.

- Resist drowning in self-doubt or getting stuck on the procrastination pot in the face of difficult tasks. An ongoing appreciation for my strengths – those things I was good at and enjoyed doing – had made me aware of the resources I always had to draw upon in any situation.

Until Olivia accused me of putting profits before the wellbeing of our people. This accusation, made by someone I deeply respected, flew in the face of everything I'd tried to build our business around, and suggested a complete failing of my personal values.

My self-identity was so threatened in this moment that I was completely hijacked by my emotions. My inner critic let loose a torrent of abuse about how could I trust and invest so much in someone who had no appreciation for all I'd done for them. Steeped in shame, I was determined to isolate myself as far away from Olivia as possible, and told her she could finish up her contract with us immediately and we'd pay out any notice owed to her. And then I spent the next day – and to be honest even a year later it can still preoccupy me – ruminating in self-doubt, questioning my leadership abilities, and wondering if Olivia had been right. I discovered my personal psychological safety skills were not portable and I wound up wasting a lot of energy, scaring our other team members, and burning the bridge on what had otherwise been a very productive and successful relationship.

I can't undo the past, but I can learn how I'd lead differently next time. For example, when I felt that lightning bolt of fear and pain, I could have used the intensity of that data as a clear sign that I needed to step back from my conversation with Olivia and sanity test her accusations with others I trusted. If Olivia was correct, I absolutely needed that feedback and to take the actions required to bring me back into alignment with my values. If Olivia was lashing out because she was struggling, I also needed that feedback to understand how best to support her and our team through the next steps.

Once my moment of fear had passed, that's exactly what I did. Although it was too late to repair the relationship between Olivia and me, it was a lesson I have benefitted from learning many times.

CARE At The "Me" Level Toolbox

SHOWING COMPASSION	EXPRESSING APPRECIATION	ENCOURAGING RESPONSIBILITY	DEMONSTRATING EMOTIONAL WISDOM
Helpful for building strengths to protect against "Social Support" risks	Helpful for building strengths to protect against "Work Design" risks	Helpful for building strengths to protect against "Work Condition" risks	Helpful for building strengths to protect against "Work Experience" risks
Hit Your Reset Button	Discover Your Strengths	Tell Yourself Not Yet	Take A Joy Break
Watch Your Language	Check Your Blind Spots	Leave Your Comfort Zone	What The Func?
Take A Time Out	Find A Daily Tah-Dah	Find The Gift	Step Back To Step Forward
Own Your Stuff	Craft Your Job	Ask For Help	Navigate Negativity Landmines
Find Your Mantra	Run An Appreciation Lap	Confess Your Screw Ups	Slow Down Your Responses

Remember you can read through the rest of this chapter to get a sense of the different evidence-based practices you can use to build personal portable psychological safety. Or, simply pick the CARE practices or tools that may offer the best support for you.

> **Mindful Moment:** Be sure to record the "Me" Level tools you'd like to experiment with in your CARE Toolbox. It may be helpful to note the name of the activity and the page number to make your tools easy to find. Remember to add the psychosocial risk you're aiming to minimize.

Compassion At The "Me" Level

Why Self-Compassion Fuels Safety

Most of us have managed to speak to someone in our lives with understanding, kindness, and encouragement. But when it comes to speaking to ourselves in the same way, too often we blame ourselves, shame ourselves, and conclude we are incapable of learning and growth. Not surprisingly, studies have found that it's impossible to feel psychologically safe when we are constantly beating ourselves up.

Far from being self-indulgent or throwing ourselves a pity party, studies have found that the expression of self-compassion activates our brain's caregiving and self-awareness systems. This helps us to gain a more balanced perspective about what is unfolding and how we want to respond and provides us with the safety we need to lower our levels of stress and anxiety. This happens through three key processes:

- The mindfulness to be aware and acknowledge when we are experiencing pain;

- The kindness to comfort and soothe ourselves in these moments; and

- The sense of common humanity that reminds us that nature wired us to be perfectly imperfect, enabling us to evolve.

How To Show Self-Compassion

The common thread through every self-compassion practice is showing up for ourselves like a wise and kind best friend. We call this "The Best Friend Test". Just as a true best friend would, the first question to always ask ourselves is: "What support do you most need right now?"

Sometimes this requires comforting ourselves as we lean into uncomfortable emotions, other times it means telling ourselves a firm "no" and turning away from danger to protect ourselves. Sometimes it entails soothing and calming our bodies when we are experiencing pain, while other times it requires figuring out what we need and giving it to ourselves. Sometimes it asks us to be accepting and validating of what is, and sometimes it means motivating ourselves to jump and make change happen.

Self-Compassion Tools To Try

- **Hit Your Reset Button:** Physical gestures can have an immediate effect on our bodies, activating the soothing parasympathetic nervous system. Try putting your hands over your heart, or simply place one hand on top of the other in a comforting way while telling yourself reassuring messages such as: "Hey, I'm here for you," and "It's okay, I've got your back." This can release the hormone oxytocin which provides a sense of security, soothes distressing emotions, and calms cardiovascular stress.

- **Watch Your Language:** Be mindful not only of what you say to yourself, but also how you say it. Using a warm and gentle, rather than a cold or harsh, tone of voice can make a huge difference in your ability to support yourself in moments of struggle. Think about what that wise and kind best friend would say to you in this moment. How would they balance your needs for sympathy, encouragement, and accountability?

- **Take A Time Out:** When you feel yourself struggling, take a few minutes for a self-compassion break. Start by taking a slow breath and noticing how your body is feeling and try to label any uncomfortable emotions you're experiencing. Then, remind yourself that you're human and just like everybody else, you're still learning. Try to be a little less judgmental and more understanding towards your situation. Finally, give yourself some kind words of encouragement such as: "I'm here for you"; or, "Just keep doing your best"; or "What help do you need?"

- **Own Your Stuff:** Try not to take on the thoughts and emotions of others as though they belong to you. This means changing "He's so disappointed in me", to just "He's so disappointed." Don't fixate, don't ruminate, and don't get stuck in other people's experiences. And likewise, try not to project your pain onto others. Just own what is yours to own and let the rest go. Ask yourself: "What do I need to let other people own in this situation? What do I need to take responsibility for myself?"

- **Find Your Mantra:** A self-compassion mantra is a reminder to be kind to yourself. It makes it easier to soften and soothe, so that instead of your negative emotions hijacking your confidence, you can remain present, engaged, and authentic as you navigate your way through what's unfolding. What would a wise and kind friend say to you in the moments you want to beat yourself up? For example: "Hang on, in most situations you're better than you think you are. Let's figure this out." Or perhaps: "You've got this. Just slow down. Take a breath." Or even: "You're doing the best you can. Just be open to the learning and keep putting one foot in front of the other." How can you remind yourself to reach for this message in the moments when your inner critic is firing up?

Appreciation At The "Me" Level

Why Appreciating Our Strengths Makes Us Feel Safe

Researchers estimate that due to the brains' natural negativity bias, most workplaces spend about 80 percent of the time focused on trying to fix weaknesses, and only 20 percent of the time building on strengths. But, pointing out faults and demanding improvements does little to calm the brains' threat-defense responses.

In contrast, having our strengths – the things we are good at and enjoy doing – appreciated and encouraged, triggers our brains' reward responses, which regulates motivation, reinforces learning, and supports our wellbeing. For example, studies have found that when we have the opportunity to do what we do best each day, we're more likely to report higher levels of confidence and self-belief, lower levels of stress and anxiety, up to six times more engagement in our work, and we are up to 18 times more likely to be flourishing.

How To Express Appreciation For Your Strengths

The good news is that at some point, we've all experienced what using our strengths can feel like. They're the moments we find ourselves looking forward to, which then completely absorb us, and leave us feeling more confident, energized, and satisfied. It is the state psychologists call "flow" and it occurs when: you have a clear goal; the appropriate level of challenge exists between the tasks you're undertaking and your neurological superpowers; and you receive regular feedback on how you're doing so you can dial your strengths up when you're underplaying, or dial your strengths down when you're overplaying them.

Unfortunately, for many of us, these moments of flow are completely accidental; a lucky set of circumstances and opportunities that allow us to do what we do best. But what if these moments didn't have to be? What if we could intentionally develop our strengths each day at work – no matter what our job descriptions said – and appreciate the best of ourselves?

Appreciation Tools To Try

- **Discover Your Strengths:** Researchers have found that most of us struggle to name our top five strengths, which makes it difficult to appreciate them. To help you, use one of the online assessment tools to identify and understand your strengths. Gallup Strengths Finder (**gallupstrengthscenter.com**) and the Strengths Profile (**strengthsprofile. com**) are paid (and free) assessments you can use. Or, we like the free, ten-minute Valus In Action (VIA) Survey (**viacharacter.org**). These tools will give you an easy way to start exploring and applying your strengths more consistently. The websites also provide a lot of information about the strengths, including details on what they are and strategies for applying them in your day-to-day life. Be sure to stick your results somewhere you can see them so you're reminded of your top strengths regularly. Then you can appreciate what you do best each day at work.

- **Check Your Blind Spots:** Ask at least five people from different contexts in your life to write down a story about a time when they've seen you really engaged, energized, and enjoying what you were doing. What was happening in this moment? Why is it so memorable for them? Which strengths did they see you using? As you review these stories, look for common themes in how your strengths showed up in your best moments. While asking and reading what people have to say may feel uncomfortable, it can be a truly enlightening and enriching experience.

- **Find A Tah-Dah:** Choose one thing on your to-do list each day and intentionally note down the strength you want to apply to make this task a little easier, and hopefully a lot more effective. This can be particularly helpful for the tasks that bore you, overwhelm you, or that you dread. Later, when you tick the task off your list with a "tah-dah", reflect on how this strength helped with the task.

- **Craft Your Job:** Write down all the tasks required in your job, then divide them into those you enjoy and those that leave you drained. Now, think about what you could do to expand the things you enjoy doing. This might involve changing the type and number of tasks you undertake (the "what" you do at work), thinking about who you spend your time with (the "who" you do your work with), or reframing the purpose of a task (the "why" you do your work). Then experiment with what's possible. Move past your own expectations of how you "should"' spend your time and find small moments — even if it's at lunchtime or just before your day starts — to use your strengths each day.

• **Run An Appreciation Lap:** At the end of each day, take a few minutes to reflect on what you discovered about your strengths. What went well today? Which of your strengths were you drawing on in these moments? Where did you struggle today? Which of your strengths might you need to dial up or down? What did you learn about using your strengths at work? How can you apply this tomorrow? Do you need any support?

Responsibility At The "Me" Level

Why Taking Responsibility Needs Safety

Studies suggest that on average most of us spend at least thirty minutes every day at work ducking and dodging accountability. Why? Because learning and growing and delivering outcomes together is often messy, uncomfortable, and can become a threat to our self-identity. But what if this didn't have to feel so personally threatening?

Professor Carol Dweck's research has found that people who willingly take responsibility for embracing new challenges, ask for help, listen to feedback, and hold themselves accountable for their failures are more likely to have what she describes as a "growth mindset". Grounded in the belief that we are each born with a certain amount of intelligence, talent, and abilities that can grow with effort and learning, this mindset helps us to move beyond our present limitations and achieve ever-higher levels of success.

How To Encourage Responsibility

Studies suggest that when we practice a growth mindset at work we collaborate better with others because we're interested in how we can learn and grow together, rather than "being the expert". We are more innovative and are inspired by others' success because we're willing to take calculated risks rather than "look smart". And, we demonstrate greater persistence and resilience in the face of challenges and setbacks because we see them as learning opportunities, rather than "career killers".

Practicing a growth mindset makes it easier for us to take responsibility for our learning, growth, and the results we deliver because, as Carol notes: "When people already know they are deficient, they have nothing to lose by trying." It doesn't mean that our failures are painless, but it does mean they don't define us. We own our problems, deal with them, learn from them, and apply this learning so we can deliver better future results. And this is how we define success.

Responsibility Tools To Try

- **Remind Yourself Not Yet:** Tune into the stories you tell yourself about what you can't do, what you've failed at, or why you're not good enough. Acknowledge that you can't do these things "yet," but recognize that with enough effort and learning, you can always keep improving your abilities. When you hear yourself say "I can't," add on the word "yet." Remind yourself that you're on a learning curve.

- **Leave Your Comfort Zone:** Each week, set at least one learning goal to build your competence in something. It might be a skill you want to gain, a task you want to master, or simply the desire to understand something better. Notice what happens as you practice, make mistakes, make adjustments, and eventually start to do better in the competence you're building. As you tackle this goal, practice letting go of the outcome, embracing your mistakes, and identifying the processes and efforts you can build upon to keep improving.

- **Find The Gift:** Your struggles always contain an invitation – albeit often unwanted – for learning and growth. When you accept the challenge as a chance to move towards the person you want to be, you can turn the sense of threat into a feeling of opportunity that helps to transform your physical, intellectual, emotional, and social responses. Ask yourself: "What is the opportunity in this struggle for learning and growth? What small actions would I feel proud to take in response to this situation?"

- **Ask For Help:** Unfortunately, 85 percent of people say they would rather depend on themselves than on others, seeing it as a mark of grit, ambition, and productivity. The reality is, however, that you're more likely to make better decisions, tap into available resources, and be more effective as a leader when you ask for help, ask for feedback, and ask for input from others. When leaders see their role as the "chief help-seeker," they set the stage for others to ask for help as well.

Try using sentence completions to make asking for help easier. For example, "I'm currently working on X, and I could use help to Y," or, "One of my urgent tasks is to X, and I need to Y," or, "My biggest hope is

X, and I need Y." By filling in these blanks, you can gain a sense of what you're working on, what you're trying to do, and something that you could ask for.

- **Confess Your Screw Ups:** Objectively note down your screw ups of the past week whilst remembering that no one is getting it right all of the time and nature wired you to be perfectly imperfect so you could learn and evolve over time. Where did you bump up against your limitations, fall short of your ideals, or outright fail? Try to get clear on where you went wrong, what the cost was of these mistakes, and what you've learned from these experiences. Tell yourself: "I'll do better next time." Then be sure to take accountability for any actions that may be required after your reflections.

Emotional Wisdom At The "Me" Level

Why Emotional Wisdom Improves Our Safety

Researcher Dr. Susan David explains that our emotions, from blinding rage to giddy joy, are our body's immediate physical responses to what is happening around us and are designed to prepare our bodies to act in particular ways. For example, joy sparks the urge to play and be creative, interest sparks the urge to explore and learn, serenity sparks the urge to savor our current circumstances, fear sparks the urge to flee, anger sparks the urge to attack, and so on.

All day, every day, our emotions provide us with incredibly valuable data. By understanding that our emotions – even the uncomfortable ones – are "information" to be interpreted, we can cultivate our emotional wisdom. This allows us to harness the energy generated from "positive" emotions, build a tolerance for being comfortably uncomfortable with "negative" emotions, and embrace the reality that our feelings of thriving and struggle fuel our resilience and support our growth. More than simply reacting to how we feel with "emotional intelligence" or "emotionally agility", "emotional wisdom" enables us to also be proactive about shaping our feelings.

How To Demonstrate Emotional Wisdom

Proactively prioritizing opportunities to experience positive emotions – like joy, gratitude, serenity, interest, hope, pride, amusement, inspiration, awe, and love — as we go about our work, is like putting money in the bank to grow. This is because the broadened mindset enabled by the experience of positive emotions seems to be the basis for the discovery of new knowledge, new alliances, and new skills. In turn, these lead to more positive emotions, that help to build our psychological, social, intellectual, and physical resources, placing us on an upward trajectory of growth.

The caution is not to force positivity or feel the need to be positive all of the time. Positive emotions are fleeting. They're going to arise and they're going to dissipate, and we need to accept that, rather than clinging or hanging on to them regardless of what is happening around us or within us.

And, while it can be tempting to suppress or distract ourselves from feelings of anxiety, fear, anger, sadness, guilt, shame, distrust, or hate, researchers have found that developing distress tolerance — being able to shift to the upside or the downside of your emotions to get the best possible outcome for the situation — can help us to become better learners, be more successful, and experience the deepest sense of wellbeing in life.

After all, emotions in themselves are neither good nor bad; it's what we do with the data they give us that really matters.

Emotional Wisdom Tools To Try

- **Take A Joy Break:** Take a moment to do something that genuinely brings a smile to your face. It might be listening to a favorite song, watching a funny YouTube clip, reading poetry you love, calling someone who always makes you laugh, going to a place that brings you peace, or playing a game that relaxes you. Try to be fully present in this moment and savor the feeling of joy.

- **Ask What The Func?** Take a moment to tune into how your body is feeling. Are your shoulders hunched? Are you breathing easily? Is your stomach swirling? Try to name the emotions you're experiencing and tune into what might be causing them and the impact they may be having on you. What triggered the emotion? What is your body trying to tell you? What action is it prompting? What is the function of this feeling?

- **Step Back To Step Forward:** When your emotions feel overwhelming, take a moment to step back: name the emotion to acknowledge what you're experiencing; normalize the feeling by remembering that uncomfortable emotions are just data your body is providing about what is unfolding; and then, when you're ready, step forward and navigate the feeling by making choices that are aligned with who you want to be in the world and then prioritize these actions.

- **Navigate Negativity Landmines:** Reflect on your typical daily routine at work and ask yourself: "Which activities or events trigger the most negativity for me?" Is it your commute? Particular meetings? Interactions with certain colleagues or clients? Once you've rounded up your emotional landmines, ask yourself: "Is this negativity necessary? Is it helpful?" Can you avoid or modify the situation to feel more positive about it? Can you be better prepared for it? Or can you change what it means or causes you to think? Could this be an unexpected learning opportunity? Play with these approaches each time a negativity landmine explodes until you feel calmer and more confident in navigating these moments.

- **Slow Down Your Responses:** When you experience a strong emotion such as anger, slow down your response so you can respectfully and appropriately respond in ways that will be most helpful for the situation. Take a few deep breaths. Then visualize your anger as a car speedometer. If you think your anger is too high in response to the situation, then take a few moments to breathe deeply, put the brakes on, and slow down your reaction. Continue to check your emotional reaction speed during the interaction.

CHAPTER 6

Building Psychological Safety At The 'We' Level

We all share the same deep psychological needs to feel respected, valued and appreciated. From the time we are born, we seek out better ways to connect, communicate and support each other because our physical and mental wellbeing depends on it.

For example, studies have found that even when people we don't know well characterize us as "dependable" or "sincere", our brain's reward system lights up. This releases a cascade of neurotransmitters, including dopamine, serotonin, and oxytocin, which help us to learn, make decisions, and motivates us to do things that benefit ourselves and others. It also lowers our levels of cortisol which helps us to recover from work-related stress.

If this is what the tepid praise of a stranger does to the brain, what happens when we exchange mutual feelings of respect, appreciation and trust with our bosses, peers, and team members? Studies show that each positive interaction helps to return the cardiovascular system back to resting levels, and that the more of these interactions we have over time, the better protected we become from the negative effects of job strain. Furthermore, studies have found that people with strong relationships at work are less likely to perceive situations as stressful in the first place.

In contrast, researchers have found that when relationships at work are strained, the brain's threat system is more likely to be triggered. This sets off the fight-or-flight stress response, creating a surge of cortisol and fearful energy that primes us for self-defence and makes us vigilant for signs that things are going poorly. As a result, our emotional and cognitive capacities tend to become exhausted, impairing our ability to learn, solve problems, and collaborate successfully.

Perhaps this explains why one study, involving over 350 employees, in sixty business units, at a financial services company, found that the greatest predictor of a team's achievement was how the members felt about one another. And why neuroscientist Lisa Barrett Feldman notes that the best thing for the nervous system is another human, and the worst thing for the nervous system is also another human!

So, how can you teach your brain to build the kind of beliefs and skills that make it safer to work alongside others?

How Psychological Safety Makes Working Together Easier

Studies suggest that the amount of time spent collaborating with others at work has increased by approximately 50 percent over the past twelve years. The good news is that when it comes to designing creative solutions, spotting errors, solving problems, and improving profitability, researchers have found we tend to do better in groups than we do individually. The bad news is that some studies suggest many groups consistently underperform on this promise due to ongoing conflict around their goals, the uneven distribution of work, collaboration overload, and competition over who will take the credit, all of which can increase psychosocial risks.

Why is working together so challenging? Researchers have found that as we interact, on an almost minute-to-minute basis, the brain gathers and interprets people's facial expressions, body movements, and language to try and understand their intentions and motivations so we can predict their future behaviours.

This mind reading ability is designed to enhance social connections and avoid the pain of social rejection quickly and automatically. It allows us to cooperate with people we trust, avoid those we don't, and to track our reputation in the eyes of others. The difficulty is that people tend to over-estimate their mind reading abilities, which often leads to social friction, contributes to psychosocial risks, and undermines psychological safety in relationships.

For example, if asked to predict how much different colleagues like us, our efforts are likely to be little better than random guesses. And, when it comes to accurately predicting if someone is lying or telling the truth, our judgments tend to be no more reliable than flipping a coin. It turns out that most of us struggle to accurately read people's minds, and yet how well we work together greatly depends on these snap judgments.

As workplace researcher Dr. Gervase Bushe explains, overconfidence in our ability to read the minds of our colleagues can bog team relationships down in "interpersonal mush". This is because, as a safety precaution, the brain often leans towards unfavorable interpretations about other people's intentions, motivations, and actions. Not surprisingly, this leads to distrust, spotty implementation, an inability to learn together, and results in higher levels of anxiety and burnout. It is the kryptonite of psychological safety.

For example, if a colleague does something that annoys you, your brain is wired to quickly try and interpret why they behaved this way and what it means for you. If you never check your interpretation with them, regardless of the story's accuracy, it becomes a lens that colors all your future encounters with this person. And, this can make working together increasingly challenging.

Researchers suggest the only way to minimize this neurological risk is to slow down the brain's judgmental mind-reading tendencies by leaning into our curiosity. Social researcher Dr. Brené Brown suggests starting with the belief that most of the time people are doing the best they can with what they have in this moment. This belief helps to calm the brain's safety precautions, so when someone says or does something that is interpreted as potentially threatening, we feel confident and kind enough to ask them about what is unfolding. This helps us both learn how to work together better.

If such a belief about other people's intentions and motivations feels unsafe for your brain, it is worth noting that few of us ever come to work with the intention of being as difficult, disappointing, or disruptive as possible. Most people show up hoping to do good work, with good people, that will have a good impact for others, so they can go home and feel proud of their efforts.

Even when things do go wrong between work colleagues, bad intentions are rarely ever the cause. Instead, our interactions are more likely to be awkward, clumsy, messy, frustrating, or painful because we're each still learning how to navigate the complex and dynamic nature of working effectively together. The best way to figure this out is to be curious as we talk openly and honestly with each other about what is happening, to ask for what we need, and to continue showing up and trying for as long as we can (see Figure 10).

In a nutshell, we demonstrate CARE for each other. We show compassion for the fact we are each perfectly imperfect. We express appreciation for the strengths we each bring to our work and our relationships. We encourage shared responsibility as we learn the best ways to work together. And, we demonstrate emotional wisdom as we give each other permission to share our feelings – even the uncomfortable ones – rather than hiding them due to embarrassment or shame.

This is how psychological safety is built in teams and how psychosocial risks can be more quickly and effectively minimized.

JUDGEMENT		CURIOSITY
Rushing To Mind-Read Assuming the worst, leaping to conclusions, and failing to check our understanding.		**Slowing Down & Asking** Assuming the best, taking a breath and asking questions to better understand.
Biting Your Tongue Assuming learning is embarrassing, we avoid conversations and fix it ourselves.		**Offering Support** Assuming learning is helpful, we speak up and offer our support to assist.
Groaning & Moaning Assuming others are incapable, we resort to complaining and rob others of growth.		**Daring & Sharing** Assuming everyone is capable, we spark a clear and kind conversation to enable growth.
Pointing The Finger Assuming others are to blame, we overly focus on mistakes and shame people.		**Sitting In Responsibility** Assuming we share responsibility, we create a safe space for each of us to be accountable.

Figure 10: "We" Level Psychological Safety Continuum

Your "We" Level Leadership Challenge

Studies have found that caring for team members is the most important thing leaders can do to create a high trust culture. The challenge is that when we take on a leadership role, levels of testosterone – the confidence and risk-taking hormone – tend to rise, which inhibits the production of oxytocin – the caring for others hormone.

Researchers suggest that this experience of power propels us forward in one of two ways: toward the abuse of power with impulsive and unethical actions, or toward benevolent behaviour that advances the greater good. The key to increasing the levels of oxytocin is to use this power to prioritize the care of others. Not only is this choice better for the wellbeing and performance of ourselves and our team, it is also more likely to ensure we are able to continue in our leadership positions.

Our actions as leaders communicate what is expected and acceptable for our teams. By prioritizing the care of others, we set the stage for psychological safety and signal that it is not enough to simply complete team tasks regardless of the human cost. It provides permission for help-seeking, help-giving, and learning to be prioritized and encourages the practices of kindness and inclusion. It also shows that extending respect and appreciation to each other is valued.

Studies have found leaders can have a significant impact on their team's levels of psychological safety by:

- **Being Inclusive** – When leaders are sensitive to people's needs and feelings, cultivate a sense of belonging, and treat everyone fairly, they create an atmosphere of trust and respect.

- **Communicating Openly** – When leaders invite and acknowledge different perspectives, listen actively, provide clear task rationales, and invest in meaningful feedback, people are more likely to feel valued and heard.

- **Providing Choices** – When leaders offer choices about what, when, and how tasks are done, share decision-making, and appreciate people's efforts, they foster a sense of control and competence.

- **Encouraging Risk Taking** – When leaders make work assignments optimally challenging, welcome new ideas and approaches, value informed risk-taking, recognize and celebrate successes, and make it safe to learn from mistakes and failures, they promote a climate of innovation and growth.

- **Addressing Conflict** – When leaders are comfortable with open dialogue, healthy debates, differing opinions, and co-creation, they create a team environment that is free from fear and mistrust, and supports collaboration.

In other words, psychological safety is improved by behaving with integrity, humility, and expressing CARE for your team. The toolbox on the following pages of this chapter is a good place to start.

Your "We" Level Team Challenge

It is important to remember that for psychological safety to exist in your team, there must be a shared belief about how team members will respond when they each put themselves on the line. This means that while you can role model and support the conditions for psychological safety to exist in your team, at the end of the day, your team members must hold similar perceptions of the support, care, and trust they are likely to receive from each other.

They must be able to:

- Ask questions of each other without the fear of being seen as ignorant.

- Ask for help and admit to mistakes without being judged as incompetent.

- Ask for feedback without being labelled as high maintenance.

- Criticize past or present events without being branded as negative.

This is especially true when team members hold varying levels of authority and influence over each other.

It is worth nothing that at the team level, psychological safety is more than just the trust one person has for another person. It is a climate that is created and characterized by the absence or presence of trust, respect, and care.

Each team member needs to feel connected and valued by their colleagues. Workplace researcher Dr. Jane Dutton and her colleagues have found when our interactions – be it a passing moment or long days spent together – are marked by positive regard, trust, and active engagement, we each feel more open, engaged, competent, and attached to each other and our workplace. As a result, the social fabric of our team strengthens psychological safety and wellbeing so that cooperation and collaboration become easier and of higher quality.

So how can you make these kinds of connections a reality across your team? In addition to your own role modelling, you need to make sure you're giving your team members the knowledge, tools, and support they need to care for each other. You can share the toolbox on the following pages, request training for your team, and encourage your team members to utilize the coaching, mentoring, and peer support programs that exist in your workplace.

Paige's Story: Embracing The Mess & Magic

Beyond what the research tells us, we understand the importance of psychological safety because we've experienced it with the teams we work with. For example, Paige and our team were asked by their CEO, Colin, to assist the executive team of a large financial services company who had discovered their day-to-day behaviours were undermining the psychological safety of each other and their organization in a recent workplace wellbeing study.

We started by observing an executive team meeting and quickly found several safety gaps between the "old" team members – many of whom, including Colin, had been with the company for more than twenty years – and the "new" team members, who had joined more recently. While the "new" team members repeatedly made suggestions to improve how the company's strategy could be executed, the "old" team members rolled their eyes and responded with variations of: "We've tried that in the past. It doesn't work for us." There was never an invitation to co-design an approach that learned from the past and took advantage of new changes.

However, it wasn't just the "new" team members who were struggling. We noticed the "old" team members wore a thinly veiled mask of politeness over passive-aggressive attitude towards each other. Nursing old wounds of having been misjudged, maligned, or exposed by their colleagues at some point in their journey to the C-suite, it was clear there was little trust left between the "old" guard.

While any open and honest discussion about their differences were avoided at all costs in team meetings, we soon learned that the "real" conversations were happening behind Colin's closed door. One-by-one we heard stories of how team members had gone to Colin to complain about their colleagues whilst trying to win support and favor for themselves. Instead of helping team members to resolve their differences together, Colin unwittingly exacerbated the team's unhealthy dynamics by hearing each person out alone.

After witnessing all of this, we understood why the wellbeing study data had reported such low scores on morale, wellbeing, and performance. The executive team were openly caught up in their grudges and disagreements, their hostilities were being felt across the company, and their behaviours were destroying any sense of shared purpose or strategy. It was a culture of suspicion and fear.

Drawing on the company's data and our observations, Paige sat down for a very honest conversation with Colin to help him make sense of what was happening and the contributing behaviours. She asked Colin if he was willing to take personal responsibility for role modelling the behaviours that would be required to begin building a culture of safety and care?

Paige explained, it would require calling a team meeting and sharing the insights in a way that demonstrated Colin's learning about the strengths and struggles unfolding in the team. It would mean not blaming the executives, but role modelling the courage to take accountability for Colin's own behaviours that had contributed to the "old" and "new" divide, the acceptance of passive aggressive politeness, and the suspicion of "favorites". And, it would depend on Colin's curiosity to openly ask, encourage, and reward the co-creation of solutions together – not behind closed doors.

There was a long and uncomfortable silence, as Colin digested what this meant practically for how he would need to lead. While this change would be implemented through the Colin's small daily actions, it was not a little ask. To support Colin, Paige would provide weekly one-on-one coaching and team coaching for the executive team so together they could learn how to create safe spaces, navigate their differences, and build a healthier future for themselves and their company.

After sleeping on it, Colin agreed and the work began. Of course, things didn't change overnight but with Paige's support, Colin kept experimenting, sharing his learnings with the executive team, and steadily improving his behaviours. And as Colin consistently encouraged more open and honest conversations and rewarded co-creation, the executive team gradually came to trust and respect each other, no matter how long they'd been on the team.

How do we know? Because in meeting after meeting, the team witnessed each other's efforts of being more curious and less judgmental. Emails were sent that expressed appreciation for each other's strengths. When mistakes were made, the executives were now willingly stepping in and up to what was theirs to own, rather than blaming others. And in conversations, rather than pretending they had all the answers, the executives were talking openly about the ups and downs of the mess and magic of leading in the complex, dynamic world we live and work in. And the company's next wellbeing study reflected the positive impact of these changes on their team's levels of psychological safety.

CARE At The "We" Level Toolbox

SHOWING COMPASSION	EXPRESSING APPRECIATION	ENCOURAGING RESPONSIBILITY	DEMONSTRATING EMOTIONAL WISDOM
Helpful for building strengths to protect against "Social Support" risks	Helpful for building strengths to protect against "Work Design" risks	Helpful for building strengths to protect against "Work Condition" risks	Helpful for building strengths to protect against "Work Experience" risks
Get Curious	Share Your Strengths	Take A Purposeful Pause	Respond Actively And Constructively
Use Code Lavender Alerts	Co-Create Job Titles	Ask SMARTly	Monitor Your Signals
Embrace Diversity	Give Strengths Feedback	Build A Boundary Checklist	Broaden Each Other's Perspectives
Share Opposing Views	Have A Strengths Check	Share The Victory Laps	Invest In Favors
Drink Coffee Together	Navigate Strength Collisions	Talk To People, Not About People	Ignite Gratitude

Remember you can read through the rest of this chapter to get a sense of the different evidence-based practices you can use to build psychological safety for your team. Or, simply pick the CARE practices or tools that may offer the best support for you to role model.

Mindful Moment: Be sure to record the "We" level tools you'd like to experiment with in your CARE Toolbox. It may be helpful to note the name of the activity and the page number to make your tools easy to find. Remember to add the psychosocial risk you're hoping to minimize.

Compassion At The "We" Level

Why Compassion Feeds Safety

If we apply the research to any given context, it is likely that every day someone in your team is struggling, and maybe even suffering. It might be the pressure of unreasonable deadlines, feeling unappreciated, navigating changes, being uncertain about the future, or the many sources of suffering outside the workplace. Whatever the reason, pain colors our feelings of safety, wellbeing, and performance at work.

When we're willing to see and acknowledge someone's struggle at work – even if we didn't cause it or can't solve it – we show compassion. It is expressed through feelings of warmth, concern, and care for another's suffering, and our motivation to help improve their wellbeing.

While we often fear that showing compassion may leave us appearing "soft" or at risk of being taken advantage of, studies have found that the most compassionate people also set the most effective boundaries. It is the ability to clearly and kindly communicate what is and is not okay that allows them to sustain their generosity with others.

How To Show Compassion

Studies have found that compassion is a four-part process that involves:

- **Noticing Suffering** – Some people can feel too embarrassed or ashamed to talk about what's causing them pain, so it's important to keep our eyes open for changes in people's usual patterns. For example, someone may look more exhausted, be more short-tempered, or seem less engaged in their work.

- **Understanding Suffering** – Ask humble and kind questions to create a safe space for someone to share their experiences. Bring care and curiosity to the conversation rather than judgment, remembering that most of the time people are doing the best they can with what they have in any given moment.

- **Feeling Empathy** – Be willing to simply listen, see things from their perspective, and express concern without rushing to try and fix things. While sitting with other people's distress can feel challenging, the brain simultaneously rewards us for caring, while decreasing the distress felt from empathizing with someone who is suffering.

- **Taking Action** – Small actions or gestures don't have to take a lot of time or energy but can make a huge difference in helping the person feel like their suffering is acknowledged. Saying sorry for what they're experiencing, continuing to check in on how they are doing, and offering help are all valuable ways to provide support.

Compassion Tools To Try

- **Get Curious:** If you can see a team member is struggling, instead of assuming they're incompetent or untrustworthy, bring your caring and curious self to the situation by asking: "What else may be happening for this person?" If you're unsure, reach out to them and kindly – without blame or judgment – ask if everything is okay, share what you're noticing, and ask if you can help in any way.

- **Use Code Lavender Alerts:** Similar to "Code Blue" alerts for medical emergencies, "Code Lavender" alerts are an easy way to signal that someone in your team is facing extreme stress or burnout. By wearing a lavender bracelet or wrist band (or adding a lavender emoji to a virtual meeting screen), team members can safely signal they are struggling and in need of support, patience, and care from their team mates.

- **Embrace Diversity:** When you interact with someone who doesn't look like you, consider what that experience is like for them. Ask yourself: "How do people who don't look like me experience me?" Would it be an experience that contributes in a positive or negative way? Does it help to build trust or erode it?

- **Share Opposing Views:** Encourage healthy debate among team members by creating safe spaces for people with different perspectives to come together to discuss fact-based ideas they are passionate about.

Consider asking them to argue each other's perspective to improve their ability to hear and learn from each other.

- **Drink Coffee Together:** Make regular times for your team to just connect and talk to each other about any topic. While this may sound inefficient, a study of one organization found that when synchronized coffee breaks were introduced, profits increased, as did employee satisfaction.

Expressing Appreciation At The "We" Level

Why Appreciating Strengths Builds Confidence

When we have opportunities to use our strengths – the things we are good at and enjoy doing – in our teams each day, studies have found that levels of engagement, performance, sense of safety, and wellbeing are all likely to be higher. In addition, using these strengths at work has been found to improve levels of job resources and lower levels of job demands which make burnout less likely.

This is because our strengths represent our neurological superpowers. We've spent so much time practicing these particular thoughts, feelings, and behaviours that we've built up neural pathways that make it easy, effective, and enjoyable to show up in these ways. As a result, opportunities to use strengths at work leave us feeling more energized, creative, confident, and resilient.

Despite the potential benefits of appreciating each other's strengths, researchers have cautioned that this can make people more vulnerable to disappointment and distress. When we've had an opportunity to use our strengths but still failed to achieve the desire result, our sense of safety and wellbeing can be threatened.

For this reason, it's important your team understands that at times we all underplay or overplay our strengths at work. Generally, when someone is lacking confidence, procrastinating, or putting things off, it's because their strengths are being underplayed. And, when they're brimming with so much confidence that they're annoying other team members, making silly mistakes, or are at risk of exhausting themselves, it's because their strengths are being overplayed. Nudging each other to dial these strengths up or down when needed, can help teams to continue safely developing their strengths as they work together.

Appreciation Tools To Try

- **Share Strengths:** Ask each team member to consider what their strengths are, what energizes them at work, and what they gravitate towards. Based on these strengths, have each person write down three things that others can come to them for when they need support. This can create new opportunities to value and appreciate what each person does best.

- **Co-Create Job Titles:** Give people the freedom to create their own job title or job description that reflects their strengths and what they do when they're in a state of flow. Start by taking a strengths survey (visit viacharacter.org), then give people the opportunity to fuse these strengths into their role by asking them: "Based on your strengths, what do you want to own in this role?" For example, a receptionist in a popular doctor's office gave herself the title of "Director of First Impressions."

- **Give Strengths-Feedback:** High performing teams have been found to give nearly six times more feedback to each other than average teams. Rather than simply saying "great job", try to be specific about the strengths a team member used, the difference this made, why it was appreciated, and how they could build on it in future. It costs only a few extra moments but has a big impact.

- **Have A Strengths Check:** Research into the practices of the best team leaders reveals that they conduct weekly check-ins with each team member about near-term work. These conversations provide clarity regarding what is expected of each team member and why, what great work looks like, and how people can do their best work in the upcoming days. Try asking: "What lit you up last week and which of your strengths were you drawing on? What are you looking forward to this week and which strengths will you build on? Is there any support you need?"

- **Navigate Strengths Collisions:** Every now and then, team members may find that their strengths have collided. For example, one person's strength of courage and another's person's strength of prudence may leave them feeling completely thwarted by each other. By identifying the different strengths that are in play for each person, and the potential value all strengths bring, it's possible to depersonalize the tension and create a bridge of respect and safety as team members find better ways to leverage each other's strengths.

Responsibility At The "We" Level

Why Responsibility Is A Team Sport

When it comes to taking responsibility, studies have found that most people struggle with accountability. This is because there is often a lack of clarity about what organizations and teams are trying to achieve, priorities frequently change, which creates confusion about ownership, deadlines don't feel like "real" commitments, and there is a belief that solving problems is "someone else's job".

A lack of clarity, confidence, and support trigger the brain's threat response system, which activates the fight-or-flight stress response. This leaves us either blaming others when our responsibilities are not met or doing our best to avoid responsibility altogether. The brain's response has also been found to increase levels of self-doubt, impair decision making, and limit our learning and growth, all of which undermines our sense of psychological safety and wellbeing.

In contrast, the brain's reward system is triggered when we have clarity about our shared purpose; we understand the importance of the actions we have been assigned; we have the resources available to support us; there is some freedom in how we can achieve the desired outcomes, and there is safety to learn together. This boosts our levels of motivation, improves critical thinking and problem solving, promotes growth, and leaves us more willing to take accountability.

When we insist on personal responsibility and collective accountability (instead of indulging incompetence, settling for half-hearted compliance, or looking the other way when boundaries and values are crossed), teams step up, learning improves, and better outcomes follow.

How To Encourage Collective Responsibility

Research has shown there are five factors that influence the likelihood of someone taking responsibility. These are:

- **Attribution** – Will others know it was mine to do?

- **Observability** – Will others see me doing/not doing it?

- **Evaluability** – Will I be judged on my actions?

- **Answerability** – Will I be asked to justify my actions?

- **Consequentiality** – Will I be rewarded or punished as a result of my actions?

The more of these factors are present, the greater degree of accountability. Unfortunately, we are too often preoccupied with the final factor alone – that of reward or punishment, which, in turn, activates the brain's threat responses. So, how might you encourage responsibility in your team?

Responsibility Tools To Try

- **Take A Purposeful Pause:** Regularly revisit your organization's purpose and goals in team meetings and ask: "How is our work making a positive difference towards these goals? Why is this important for us and the people our workplace helps? What does this mean for our priorities and the ways we're working right now? Are we confident we can deliver on these responsibilities?" Allow each person to share their own answers to these questions so they understand the value of the work they do, their current priorities, and can request any help they need to successfully deliver on their commitments.

- **Ask SMARTly:** Research suggests that clarity of expectations is one of two critical factors that drive accountability success. Once we are clear about and agreed on what needs to happen, we can get on with doing it more effectively. Make your requests SMART by being: Specific rather than general; Meaningful about why this action matters; Action oriented about the outcomes required. Realistic about available resources. Timed with clear deadlines.

- **Build A Boundaries Checklist:** Invite your team to co-create a set of clear rules about how they want to work together. Begin by making a list of what's working well when it comes to how tasks are assigned, executed, delivered, and learned from together. Then – without blaming or shaming each other – make a second list of where your team is struggling when it comes to successfully delivering and growing together. Finally, use these lists to agree on what is okay and what isn't okay when it comes to taking responsibility for the work you do together. Consider how you will kindly and respectfully nudge and support each other if someone is struggling with these commitments.

- **Share The Victory Laps:** Try to build rewards around collective, rather than individual, achievements in your team. For example, providing the opportunity for peer-to-peer rewards for collaboration, co-creation, help-giving, help-seeking, feedback, and shared learning, allows your team to recognize and reward each other's willingness to take responsibility.

- **Talk To People, Not About People:** One of the pillars of Netflix's culture is that if people have a problem with a colleague, they are expected to talk about it openly with that person rather than groan or moan to others. Holding people to this standard of transparency puts the clamp on politicking and backstabbing, flushes out the differences of opinions, and improves safety.

Emotional Wisdom At The "We" Level

Why Emotional Wisdom Ripples Across Teams

Our brains are wired to synchronize with each other as we interact. For example, neuroscientist Dr. Uri Hasson's studies have found that when we connect with someone – even if they are a stranger – the mirroring of emotions across our brain is widespread. For example, when we see someone smiling, our mirror neurons for smiling are activated, which makes us feel like we're smiling too.

What might this mean for the ways we work together? When the brain mirrors facial expressions, body language, speech patterns, and verbal tones, our emotions have the potential – depending on the emotion, the energy with which it is expressed, and our susceptibility to contagion – to spread and shape team dynamics and outcomes, as seen in Chapter 5.

For example, pleasant mood contagion in teams has been associated with greater cooperation, less conflict, and more complex logical reasoning and problem solving. This is in contrast to unpleasant mood contagion which has been associated with less cooperation, rejection of others, and increased risk of burnout.

Researchers have found that the process of emotional contagion is usually so subtle, team members often don't realize it is occurring or the impact it is having on the way they work together. This can leave them unable to tap into a powerful resource that can fuel or drain their feelings of safety and care.

How To Foster Emotional Wisdom

Dr Barbara Fredrickson's research has discovered that it takes just a micro-moment of genuine connection to spark an upward spiral of pleasant emotions and mutual care among team members. Her research suggests it takes three simple steps:

- The sharing of a positive emotion, such as interest, joy, amusement, or pride;

- The synchronization of our biochemistry and behaviours through either shared eye contact, or matching body gestures or vocal tone;

- A reflective motive to invest in each other's wellbeing that brings about feelings of warmth and trust.

She describes this process as "positivity resonance", suggesting it is like a mirror. We mirror the positivity in each other's emotional state; we mirror each other's body and brain activity patterns; we mirror each other's impulse to safely care for one another.

Emotional Wisdom Tools To Try

- **Respond Actively And Constructively:** When someone shares good news, slow down and ask them questions to help savor their good fortune and to gain more information about their experience. Show genuine interest and excitement for that person. When we are around people who are happy, excited, and energized, those feelings flow onto us, and we can't help but feel the same.

- **Monitor Your Signals:** Team members will feel they have permission to disagree by observing how you, as a leader, emotionally respond to dissent and bad news. Accommodating and encouraging it, rather than getting defensive or shutting it down, can send a clear signal that differing opinions are okay. And in doing so, it becomes a cultural norm in your team.

- **Broaden Each Other's Perspectives:** Often when people experience negative emotions, they're intensely motivated to share their experience with others. People want their feelings validated, to know that others care, and to get help in thinking through what happened as it can be difficult to do this on their own. However, there's an art to providing good support to others. It's not as simple as just talking, nodding your head, or simply agreeing, which can sometimes lead to co-rumination or vent sessions that fuel more anger, sadness, or anxiety. Instead, show care and validate their experience by learning about what they went through. When there is enough context to understand the difficulty, try to help them gain some distance and broaden their perspective.

- **Invest In Favors:** Encourage your team to spend five minutes each day helping someone else in their team or networks. Dr. Adam Grant suggests thinking of this as a "five-minute favor". Your team could share information, connect contacts, offer feedback, or make a recommendation that helps others. If people offer to repay your team in some way, ask them to pay it forward by helping or supporting someone else.

- **Ignite Gratitude:** To help weave gratitude into the fabric of your team, create a peer-to-peer recognition system. This doesn't have to be complicated or expensive, just a simple way for your team members to express their appreciation for each other. Help your team move from the specific, discreet instances of gratitude to a more fundamental, grateful culture and grateful way of life. Finding ways to make gratitude a habit, so that it eventually becomes a more integrated and automatic practice, can have a much bigger impact.

CHAPTER 7

Building Psychological Safety At The "Us" Level

Every workplace aspires to having a healthy – rather than toxic – culture. Studies have repeatedly found healthy workplace cultures foster employee commitment, lower risks, improve productivity, enhance brand reputation, and support an organization's overall success and sustainability. These benefits have a bottom-line effect of reducing costs and increasing revenue. As a result, data-driven financial analysts acknowledge culture is a critical factor for long-term financial success and seventy-nine percent of Fortune 1000 CEO's and CFO's view culture as one of the top three factors affecting their firm's value.

Why might this be the case? Because culture is the glue that binds the ways we work together. When a culture is healthy, it focuses and energizes people around achieving an organization's mission and strategic goals. It shapes personal priorities and helps to co-ordinate behaviour by emphasizing what is valued and rewarded. A strong culture also helps to reduce complexity and provides continuity by guiding how things are done – or not done – in a workplace.

Studies have found that because culture is a product of accumulative beliefs, values, norms, and practices, it is never static. It is lived and breathed with each decision, conversation, and action taken or not taken at the "Me",

"We", and "Us" levels. For example, it can be heard in the ways people talk to each other – are they open and honest or withholding and lying? It can be seen in the ways team members treat each other – are they caring and respectful or ruthless and abusive? And, it can be felt in our interactions with each other – are they supportive and collaborative or non-inclusive and cutthroat?

Culture is also shaped by what is unfolding in the world around our workplaces. The changing needs of stakeholders, economic circumstances, and political environment can all impact culture. This can be seen in the shifts the Great Recession, the global pandemic, or Black Lives Matter created across workplaces in recent years. And, changes in industry and legal requirements, such as the introduction and strengthening of codes and legislation for minimizing psychosocial hazards, reshape our cultures.

So, how do safety and care contribute to healthy workplace cultures?

How Cultures Of Safety And Care Are Built

Dr. Jennifer Chatman and her colleagues suggest healthy cultures are created through a blend of:

- **Values** that define what is important and why it matters;
- **Norms** that define the beliefs and behaviours that are widely shared and supported;
- **Accountability** that is actively encouraged and rewarded.

Why Healthy Cultures Value Safety

While values vary enormously between organizations, studies have found that workplaces who develop healthy cultures, regardless of their age, size, or industry, consistently share one value: the promotion of innovation and change. Realizing this value depends on team members having the beliefs and behaviours that it is safe to ask questions, seek feedback, experiment, reflect on results, and discuss errors or unexpected outcomes. It requires the norms of psychological safety.

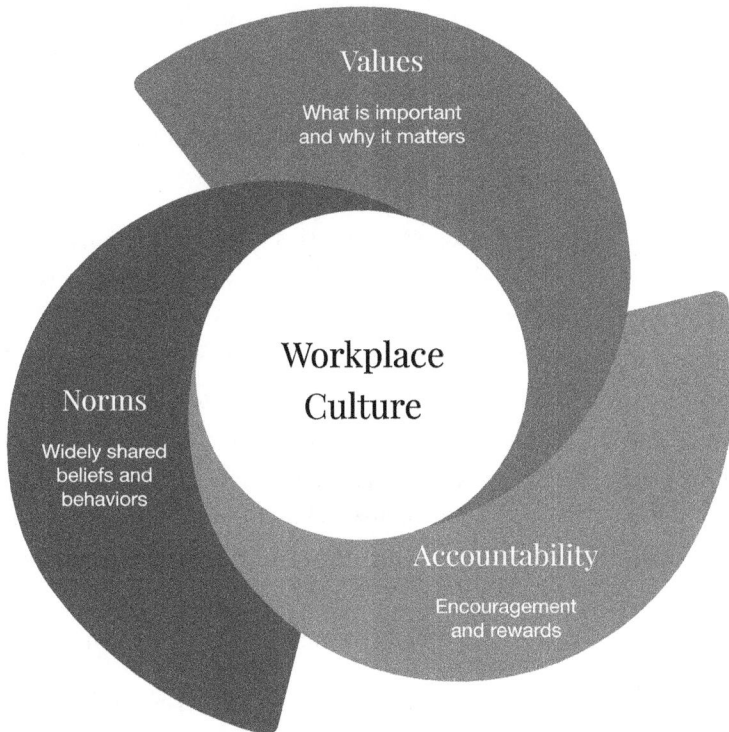

Figure 11: Workplace Culture Components

How Norms Guide Care

While formal workplace rules are useful for addressing situations that are predictable and regular, norms help us to interpret and navigate situations that are nearly impossible to anticipate and difficult to solve. They are the unwritten rules about what is okay and isn't okay as we work together.

For example, luxury department store Nordstrom is famous for its culture of outstanding customer service. To help realize this and make it a norm, Nordstrom workers learn on day one "to use their best judgment" so they can take creative action without asking for permission to solve customer issues. When a customer found Nordstrom didn't have the shoes she wanted in her size, one of the sales associates found what she needed online at Macy's (their competitor), ordered the shoes to be shipped overnight, and paid for the shipping.

Studies suggest one of the most effective ways to encourage norms of safety and care at the "Us" level is by providing a supportive organizational environment through workplace systems (i.e., human resources, risk management, internal communication, technology platforms, etc.). For example, researchers found that when an organization's human resources practices signal a long-term investment in a mutually respectful relationship with its people, norms that support a social climate of safety and care emerge. By investing in practices such as diversity and inclusion, providing training to improve team communication and interactions, focusing performance appraisals on strengths development, and basing compensation on cultural contributions, workplaces can demonstrate a commitment to their values.

The good news is that the CARE Toolbox you've been building already contains small evidence-based practices to help shape the values, norms, and accountability of your culture of safety and care at the "Me" (Chapter 5) and "We" (Chapter 6) levels from a bottom-up approach. When your organizational practices at the "Us" level – often led by your CEO, executive leadership group and human resource teams – are also aligned, then your culture of safety and care is significantly more likely to flourish.

How Accountability Demonstrates Safety & Care

Remember, the brain lights up with pleasure when we co-operate and help each other and lights up with pain when we feel excluded or rejected. This is why the values and norms of workplaces have been found to be more effective at controlling behaviours than either monetary rewards or physical work environments, provided accountability is encouraged.

For example, our Nordstrom customer didn't start out having an exceptional experience. The first sales associate who served her – Lance – simply apologized that the size she wanted wasn't available in the store. It wasn't until a second sales associate – Howard –intervened to enact the norm of "use your best judgment" that this memorable moment of customer service was created.

Then, as the customer was leaving, she accidently overheard Howard telling Lance: "I can't believe you didn't work harder to find those shoes for her. You really let us down." Howard wasn't Lance's boss – they were peers – but in this second memorable moment, he demonstrated that commitment to the norms of customer service are so strong at Nordstrom, team members are willing to sanction each other, regardless of status, for failure to uphold the norms.

Leaders and team members play a vital role in socializing each other to the shared values and norms. By clarifying what is and isn't okay as they work together, and quickly providing each other with feedback when values and norms are violated, we strengthen psychological safety and role model care.

As leaders, we need to talk in ways that show our team how their strategic priorities and daily actions help to uphold organizational values. We need to highlight and reward examples of team members who are successfully applying these norms. And, we need to quickly flag violations of our shared values and norms and encourage self-correction – especially if we are the person who has broken the rules.

We also need to provide feedback to more senior leaders about the organizational practices that undermine the workplace's values and norms and suggest alternative approaches that helps everyone to better walk the organizational talk.

Atlassian's Story: Building A Culture Of Psychological Safety

Australian software company Atlassian is known for its unique and innovative approach to collaboration, transparency, and employee empowerment. Built on its shared beliefs that "behind every great human achievement there is a team", the company's culture of safety and care creates an environment where everyone feels valued, supported, and empowered to do their best work.

To guide their desired culture, the company's founders, employees, and stakeholders came together and agreed a shared set of values:

- Open Company, No Bullshit

- Build With Heart And Balance

- Don't F@! percent The Customer

- Play, As A Team

- Be The Change You Seek

To create widely shared cultural norms for these values, Atlassian intentionally uses its organizational support practices to demonstrate their commitment to living these values. For example:

- **Structure** – Atlassian has an almost completely flat management structure and encourages teams to self-organize around customer needs and take ownership of their work.

- **Recruitment** – Atlassian has a policy of "no jerks" which requires them to pass on hiring people who may be exceptionally talented and capable, but don't share the company's values. Candidates who pass this test and are hired, receive a little care package before they even sign a contract. And, once someone becomes an official employee they are provided with a "holiday before you start" travel voucher to show them that Atlassian cares about their welfare.

- **Communication** – Atlassian has an open-door policy (and "virtual" open door meetings for people working remotely) that allows employees to communicate directly with the company's leaders. Access to information about the company's goals, financials, operations, and every project are provided to all employees. For example, the entire company knew they were going public four months before Atlassian filed.

- **Team Meetings** – At the beginning of each meeting, everyone has the mic for two minutes to share what's top of mind from a personal perspective and a minute on what's top of mind from a business perspective.

- **Feedback** – Atlassian holds "design crits" to share ideas, encourage healthy debate, and welcome feedback. They support "safe-to-fail" low-risk experiments to test new ideas, conduct blame-free post-mortems on all large projects, and have a "Fail Stories" program for employees to share their failures and what they learned from them with their colleagues.

- **Development Opportunities** – "Shipit Days are Atlassian's spin on Google's idea of allowing its people to spend 20 percent of their time on their own ideas. With Shipit Days, Atlassian gives its people four 24-hour slots per year to dedicate to their own ideas.

- **Retrenchment** – When the company recently cut 500 jobs, representing five percent of its global workforce, Atlassian provided impacted workers with ongoing access to their work tools, the time and support to say goodbye to their colleagues, and a 15-week separation package, plus one week for every year of service.

Understanding the importance leaders in building accountability, Atlassian provides training, playbooks, tools, peer feedback, and recognition of leaders who embody the company's values and norms. As a result, Atlassian is known for its culture of safety and care and has repeatedly been recognized as one of Australia's best places to work.

CARE At The "Us" Level Toolbox

SHOWING COMPASSION	EXPRESSING APPRECIATION	ENCOURAGING RESPONSIBILITY	DEMONSTRATING EMOTIONAL WISDOM
Helpful for building strengths to protect against "Social Support" risks	Helpful for building strengths to protect against "Work Design" risks	Helpful for building strengths to protect against "Work Condition" risks	Helpful for building strengths to protect against "Work Experience" risks
Be Purpose Driven	Coach Leaders	Honor Commitments	Give What You Can
Invest In Values	Hire For Strengths	Confront Performance Problems	Celebrate Rites Of Passage
Ask For Help	Invest In Strengths Development	Get What You Pay For	Embrace Fun
Make Helping Fun	Redesign Jobs	Provide Air Cover	Deliver Negative Stuff Personally
Encourage Kindness	Invite Flash Mentoring	Audit Your Culture	Think About Others

Remember, you can read through the rest of this chapter to get a sense of the different evidence-based practices you can use to build organizational support for psychological safety. Or, simply pick the CARE practices or tools that may offer the best support for your workplace.

> **Mindful Moment:** Be sure to record the "Us" level tools you'd like to recommend to your workplace or experiment with yourself in your CARE Toolbox. It may be helpful to note the name of the activity and the page number to make the tools easier to find. Don't forget to add the psychosocial risk the tool may help to minimize.

Compassion At The "Us" Level

Why Compassion Requires Safety

When it comes to getting ahead in workplaces, is it a case of survival of the fittest or the survival of the kindest? While most organizations are fuelled by a fierce competitive spirit that drives us to work faster, harder, and better than others, studies suggest that over time competition undermines performance.

Researchers have found that while we're all competitive to some extent, we also need high levels of trust and helpfulness – which competition tends to corrode – to perform at our best. This is because when we're working hard to survive the competitive aggression of others, our focus narrows and productivity tends to decline. It turns out the most productive workplaces are characterized by giving and receiving help from others.

How To Make Compassion A Norm

Organizational researcher Dr. Adam Grant explains that while people are inherently generous, their beliefs about the types of social interactions a workplace values shapes just how generous they will be with each other. For example, in a culture where people are forced to compete for scarce resources, generosity is discouraged in favor of being "takers" who get as much as they can from others, or "matchers" who constantly try to ensure an even exchange of favors, to ensure their own success.

In contrast, in a culture where people feel supported and valued for behaving generously and caring about others, they are more likely to behave as "givers" who willingly share their time, energy, knowledge, skills, ideas, and connections to benefit others. Studies have found that when a culture of generosity is prioritized, people are more efficient at solving problems, getting work done, and balancing workloads to ensure consistent performance. They are also more likely to build teams that are cohesive and coordinated and establish environments in which others feel their needs are the top priority. As a result, the workplace and the people in it are more likely to flourish.

Compassion Tools To Try

- **Be Purpose Driven:** Try to find ways to help your people regularly embody your organization's purpose as they go about their work. When people pursue a challenging purpose together, the sense of ego-driven isolation begins to dissolve and they recognize their interdependence. But purpose can't just exist inside a company report. It's something that lives inside your people and requires their active participation. For example, one bank has a purpose to make banking joyful. So, each team meeting at the bank begins with a quick conversation about what the team are going to do to make the banking experience joyful this week, for customers and each other, to bring that purpose to life.

- **Invest In Values:** If your organization hasn't already done so, name your safety and care values. This can be done in your team or across your entire organization by bringing stakeholders together and asking them to help identify the three to five most important workplace values when it comes to achieving your shared purpose in ways that support safety and care. Once these values are defined, ask your people to help clarify the safety and care behaviours that support each value, the behaviours that undermine it, and examples of when the value has been practiced. Then agree how you will help to hold each other and your organization accountable to living these values each day.

- **Ask For Help:** Studies have found that ninety percent of help is given in response to requests for assistance. The challenge is that most people are reluctant to ask. Try holding a daily ten-minute stand-up meeting for your team to check in each morning with the following questions: "What did you work on yesterday? What are you working on today? And what support do you need?" Make it mandatory that people ask for support from someone in the team. While people may initially ask for small and safe things, over time their sense of safety, confidence, and generosity will grow, and people will ask for bigger and more important things. Encouraging people to ask for help is a great way to fuel emotional, relational, and organizational energy and build psychological safety.

- **Make Helping Fun:** Can you use hackathons, challenges, or mini-games to incentivize people to tap into the resources that exist in their network to help solve complex business problems? For example, one company used a mini-game to reward their people for increasing the company's social media activity. Goals were set, rewards were offered, but as many of their people didn't know how to share posts or tweets, the game prompted them to ask for help from each other. As a result, not only did their social postings grow, but their ability to ask each other for help also improved considerably.

- **Encourage Kindness:** Create opportunities for your organization and your people to demonstrate kindness and support for each other outside of work. For example, The Motley Fool – a finance and investment company – have a "Fool in Need" program where employees voluntarily contribute a couple of dollars each pay period to a pool of funds to help their colleagues. Then when team members need financial support – for example to care for a sick relative, to fund a child's learning opportunity, etc. – people can apply to the fund which is overseen by three senior leaders to ensure confidentiality and accountability for how the funds are distributed.

Appreciation At The "Us" Level

Why Appreciating Strengths Needs Organizational Support

Workplace values and norms reflect our inherent beliefs about people. Do we believe that generally people can't be trusted to do their best work and need to have their weaknesses repeatedly identified and corrected? Or, do we believe that generally people are doing the best work they can and need opportunities and support to continue developing their strengths?

Studies have found that when workplaces focus on their people's strengths and embed this into their values and norms, levels of engagement, sales, and profitability increase and there is a significant reduction in safety incidences and staff turnover. This is because when employees believe they are being provided with opportunities to identify, develop, and use their strengths at work, they are more likely to feel positive, perform better, be more innovative, and behave in ways that are more supportive and altruistic towards each other.

How can workplaces provide more strengths-development opportunities? Researchers suggest that human resources practices like role descriptions, recruitment, training and development, task allocation, and feedback appraisals, are an essential organizational support to build strengths-focused cultural norms.

How To Appreciate Strengths

Studies suggest strengths-focused human resources practices need to support the following norms:

- **Knowing Strengths** – Building a shared language to talk about strengths builds a deep conceptual, practical, and collective understanding, as well as a personal understanding of each person's unique strengths profile.

- **Seeing Strengths** – Shifting perspectives to look for the best within every individual by spotting strengths' synergies, collisions, and potential – intra-personally, inter-personally, and in teams – reinforces the belief that people are trying to do their best work.

- **Applying Strengths** – Proactively aligning people's strengths to their job responsibilities, intentionally activating specific strengths to achieve individual and shared goals, and providing regular strengths-focused feedback ensures daily opportunities and encouragement for people to do their best work.

Appreciation Tools To Try

- **Coach Leaders:** Knowing, seeing, and being to apply their strengths to their roles should be a requirement for every leader. Without this foundation, your leaders will find it difficult to spot the strengths in their team, align people's tasks to their strengths, and provide strengths feedback which studies have found differentiates top-performing leaders and doubles their likelihood of success. Make sure you have invested in the necessary training and ongoing coaching your leaders need to be strengths-focused.

- **Hire For Strengths:** By shifting the focus from what people can do (competency-based recruitment) to what they are naturally good at and love doing (strengths-based recruitment), companies have reported a 50 percent drop in staff turnover, a 20 percent increase in productivity, and a 12 percent increase in customer satisfaction within a matter of months. Are you clear on the different strengths each role requires? Have these strengths been included in the role description and job advertisements? Do interview questions focus on understanding the strengths people are committed to developing, or are they focused on interrogating the weaknesses that will need fixing? Try to make sure you're hiring the strongest candidate, not the person with the least weaknesses.

- **Redesign Jobs:** Studies have found the most powerful predictors of retention, performance, engagement, resilience, and inclusion do not include pay, liking your colleagues, or even a strong belief in the mission of an organization. It is the opportunity to spend at least twenty percent of the time doing what we're good at and love doing at work. When people are struggling to perform well, it is often because their jobs are not aligned to their strengths. Rather than blaming individuals, ask: "How is this role aligned with your strengths? What can we do to make better use of your strengths in this role? What support do you need to continue developing your strengths?" And then provide the coaching and feedback workers need to see if a better alignment can be achieved.

- **Invest In Strengths Development:** Researchers have found that rating people annually on a list of competencies is a flawed method for trying to improve performance. Instead of using traditional performance management systems, they recommend investing in strengths development systems that: provide real-time feedback; offer strengths-focused coaching and course correction; and track and celebrate each person's progress throughout the year. How is your performance management system demonstrating your workplace's investment in developing your people's strengths?

- **Invite Flash Mentoring:** Mentors play a pivotal role in providing opportunities for people to see how different strengths can be used and developed across your workplace. Flash mentoring can allow your people to select someone who strengths they value and want to learn from and spend a few hours with them seeing how their strengths are applied as they go about key tasks. This quick mentoring opportunity is a great way to build connections across a workplace or team and provide practical real-world demonstrations of strengths in actions.

Responsibility At The "Us" Level

Why Responsibility Works Best As A Norm

While ensuring fairness in workplaces may feel like an impossible task, studies have found the extent to which people perceive decisions to be fair can account for twenty percent of the differences in their productivity. This is because fairness lights up the same reward circuits in the brain as winning money.

Fairness is essential for building trust. When accountability systems are seen as fair, researchers suggest that people are four times more likely to be honest (especially about their mistakes), to act fairly toward others, and serve the organization's purpose instead of their own interests.

How To Encourage Organizational Responsibility

Rather than calling for accountability after deadlines are missed or mistakes are made, researchers recommend building the following cultural norms for fairness and accountability:

- **Clear Expectations** – Help people to be crystal clear about what is expected. This means being clear about the outcome required, how success will be measured, and how the task should be approached. These expectations should be set through consultation and co-creation so people understand and feel ownership of what has been agreed.

- **Clear Capability** – Do people have the skills and resources required to meet the expectations? If not, what support can be provided? Or, how do the expectations need to be shared or adjusted? Don't set people up for unnecessary failures.

- **Clear Measurement** – Agree on weekly milestones that are tangible (i.e., work products, numerical targets, etc.) and can be reported. Consider how progress towards these milestones will be communicated (i.e., email, conversation, dashboard, etc.) as engagement and confidence are sustained by ongoing progress.

- **Clear Feedback** – As we've now learned, honest, open, ongoing feedback is critical. People need to know where they stand. Is the person delivering on their commitments? Are they working well with other stakeholders? How are new skills being learned? The feedback should go both ways — do they have the support they need? Give people the opportunity to practice accountability.

- **Clear Consequences** – There are three final choices: repeat, reward, or release. Repeat the steps above if there is still a lack of clarity in the process. If the person succeeded, reward them appropriately (acknowledgement, promotion, etc.). If they are unwilling to be accountable, despite the clarity and support provided, and there are no extenuating circumstances (i.e. illness) then it is likely they are not a good fit for the role, and should be released from it (i.e., change roles, fire them, etc.).

Accountability Tools To Try

- **Honor Commitments:** Encourage the cultural norm of people doing what they say they are going to do. Whether it is in one-on-one conversations, team meetings, or gatherings of your entire workplace, make it a habit to ask: "How did you go doing what you said you were going to do?" This way accountability becomes embedded across your organization.

- **Confront Performance Problems:** When performance problems aren't addressed, they are condoned. When performance issues arise, make it a cultural norm to hold people accountable privately and respectfully. Give people a clear choice to respect your cultural requirements or find a new opportunity. The one thing they won't do is retire on the job because it's no longer an option.

- **Get What You Pay For:** Don't just pay people for their performance, pay them for their contributions to your culture. If you have formal control over people's compensation, ensure it is aligned to behaviours that support your culture. If you have control over informal rewards (i.e., lunches, gift certificates, celebrations, etc.) for your team, use these to recognize small wins that are consistent with the desired culture. These can be effective ways of capturing people's attention about what is and isn't valued.

- **Provide Air Cover:** Don't expect others to start speaking up and offering new ideas if leaders aren't modelling this behaviour first. Encourage leaders to demonstrate vulnerability and fallibility and show people that candor is valued and appreciated. Then, if people respectfully express dissenting views or different ideas, protect them. Reduce the risk of ridicule by thanking those who do. As dissent is accommodated, this norm becomes a cultural expectation.

- **Audit Your Culture:** Role model accountability by investing in a cultural audit to understand how your organizational norms are shaping safety and care. Start by understanding and assessing your current cultural norms. Then consider what the norms would be if you were really building a culture of safety and care. Are there gaps between what you have and what you need? What behaviours might close these gaps (use your CARE Toolbox to help)? How could you socialize, orient, and train people? What would leaders be doing? What stories would you tell? How would you reward people?

Emotional Wisdom At The "Us" Level

Why Emotional Wisdom Shapes Cultures

Researchers have found that over time, patterns of emotions are repeated so often in teams that they shape the emotional culture of workplaces. These patterns tend to lean towards specific common emotions that are either positive – such as joy and care – or negative – such as anger and fear. These are expressed through cultural norms and guided by cultural values that encourage the expression – or suppression – of these emotions.

For example, in an emotional culture of anxiety, expressing worry and apprehension is not only acceptable but expected. Anxious glances, frequent disclosures about work-related worries, and commonplace conversations about the work environment that make people nervous are likely to be the norms. Through emotional contagion and feedback loops these norms can exacerbate high levels of anxiety and increase the risk of burnout as people feed off each other's nervous energy.

In contrast, an emotional culture of care (referred to by researchers as "companionate love") is evidenced by friendly eye-contact, deep listening in conversations, and offers of support for each other. As people feed off each other's feelings of care, an upward positive cycle emerges that not only helps to build safety but has also been found to help reduce anxiety and lower burnout.

How To Encourage Emotional Wisdom

Workplace policies and practices can be a surprisingly effective way to foster norms that support an emotional culture of care. For example, in some companies, employees can forego vacation days or organize emergency funds to help fellow employees who are struggling and need help.

Just as important are the small moments we prioritize that allow people to connect as human beings, and not just as "workers". For example, former Cisco CEO, John Chambers, asked that he be notified within 48 hours if a close member of an employee's family passed away so he could personally reach out to them. Former Pepsi Co. CEO, Indra Nooyi, wrote hundreds of personalized notes to the mothers, fathers, and spouses of her team members thanking them for sharing the time of the person they loved with the company and why the person was so important to the team.

Emotional Wisdom Tools To Try

- **Give What You Can:** Cycles of kindness and gratitude create a glow of goodwill among people and builds trust. What could be achieved in your organization—and what giving norms would develop—if groups of people got together weekly for thirty minutes to make requests and help one another fulfill them? Reciprocity Rings bring groups of fifteen to thirty people together and invites each person to present a request to the group members, who make contributions using their knowledge, resources, and connections to help each other.

- **Celebrate Rites Of Passage:** It's worth making a big deal of significant life events, rituals, and rites of passage, such as marriages, birthdays, deaths, and employment anniversaries, in workplaces. When stuff happens, people need opportunities to relish it together, lighten each other's loads, and console alongside others. For example, Edmunds (an automotive company) has a weekly ritual called Cadillac Catch-Up that recognizes work anniversaries, births, new employees, retirements, and other life events, often in pictures (especially for the more photogenic subjects: babies).

- **Embrace Fun:** Laughter is not just laughter; it's the most fundamental sign of safety and connection. Social extracurriculars may appear contrary to "real" work but forming meaningful relationships and deep social bonds are fail-safe measures against team breakdowns and are essential for high team performance. Summer barbecues, cheesy-Hawaiian-shirt days, holiday parties, cook offs, sporting events, and other opportunities to have fun together can help your workplace build cultural norms of belonging and care.

- **Deliver Negative Stuff Personally:** If negative news or feedback needs to be delivered, make it a norm to do so face-to-face. This rule is not easy to follow (it's far more comfortable for both the sender and receiver to communicate electronically), but it works because it deals with tension in an up-front, honest way that avoids misunderstandings and creates shared clarity and connection.

- **Think About Others:** Support the donation of time and money to charitable giving and community service. Volunteering not only helps the recipients of aid; it positively affects the volunteers as well, fostering greater psychological wellbeing and job satisfaction. For example, at Atlassian, employees are encouraged to use up to five days of paid time off per year to volunteer for charitable causes, and grants are provided to support employee-led social impact projects.

PART IV

SUSTAINING DETERMINATION

"The intention is not to develop a project with a beginning, a middle, and an end, but to create a new way of thinking, learning, communicating, working, and innovating that becomes so embedded into the organization it changes the culture."

Molly McGuigan and C.J. Murphy

When it comes to building a culture of safety and care, our research has repeatedly found that it is the frequency with which we engage in our chosen practices that shapes the values, norms, and accountability of our workplaces. For example, even when leaders only *sometimes* express compassion, appreciation, responsibility, and emotional wisdom, team members still report higher levels of safety, wellbeing, and performance. However, if we want to supercharge these outcomes, the data is clear that as leaders we need to be *often* engaging in these actions. The rhythm of how we enact and support our values, norms, and accountability are ultimately what shape our culture.

But how can you possibly find the energy, time, and resources to *often* use the CARE tools you've now chosen?

Having helped thousands of workplaces and leaders navigate this challenge, we've found the tools you've chosen can be integrated into your existing ways of working. For example, at the "Me" level, you can use your role modeling, at the "We" level your team's social rituals and current work routines can be leveraged, and at the "Us" level your organizational rules can help to embed beliefs and behaviours. In our experience, it is rarely the case that you need to add more actions to your never-ending leadership to-do list. Instead, this an opportunity to work safer (and smarter!) rather than harder.

That said, it is important to remember that feelings of safety and care are complex and dynamic. They ebb and flow based on the choices you and your team make each day, and what is happening in the world around you. As leaders, we must remain aware of what is unfolding for our team members, continually assess and prioritize what effective actions can be taken and stay curious and open to learning as our team's needs and context change.

Effectively navigating this daily ebb and flow of awareness, action, and learning cannot be rigidly managed if long-term commitment, rather than compliance, is our goal. Instead, we find it helpful to teach leaders how to design a "dynamic map" that gives them the freedom and flexibility to experiment, learn, and adapt as required. It is designed to help you let go of any lingering desires to "manage" your team and instead be fully present to the opportunities and possibilities to *often* express care for them.

To help you, we've created a "Safety & CARE Dynamic Map" to integrate your CARE Toolbox into the role modelling, routines, rituals, and rules your team already uses. And in Chapter 8, we'll guide you through a series of questions to help you plan the actions you want to implement for your team. Then, we'll show you how you can sustain the energy, motivation, and commitment to deliver your desired outcomes.

You can download an editable PDF of the "Safety & CARE Dynamic Map" to use as you read the next chapter here: **www.theleaderslab.net/leadersblue printresources.**

Safety & CARE Dynamic Map

Role Modelling
How will I show up?

Your Safety & CARE Priorities:

Routines
What does the business need?

Rules

How does our workplace guide us?

Rituals

What does my team need?

CHAPTER 8

Creating Your Safety & CARE Dynamic Map

Workplace cultures reflect the shared values and norms to which we are willing to be accountable at the "Me", "We", and "Us" levels. They are shaped by the daily rhythms of our interactions which constantly move us either towards or away from the culture of safety and care we want to be creating.

When it comes using the CARE tools we've chosen to try and influence these behaviours and interactions, researchers have found that we tend to set goals that are too big, go at them too hard, and demand results too quickly. Then, when we struggle to create the changes we want, we blame ourselves or our teams for a lack of motivation and willpower. At this point, most leaders tend to give up instead of seeking out the knowledge, tools, and support they need to make change easier.

Studies suggest these common challenges for creating behaviour changes can be avoided by aligning:

- **Motivation** – This is the desire to make change happen. When we prioritize actions because we "want to", rather than simply because we "have to", "should do", or are "expected to", it increases levels of motivation. This is why compliance will only ever get us so far when it comes to safety. Instead, be clear on *why* the CARE tools you've chosen are meaningful for you and your team. This should come from the shared language and evaluation you've gathered.

- **Ability** – This is the capability to execute chosen actions. By starting small, we set ourselves up for success. Small actions are easier to fit into busy days and they build our confidence and grow our capabilities over time, leading to bigger actions if needed. Rather, than starting with big CARE actions that will be hard to consistently implement, choose small actions that will be easy to execute and sustain. These should come from your CARE Toolbox.

- **Prompts** – This is a nudge that makes the chosen actions happen. New behaviours require a lot of energy to fire up the brain and body to move in unfamiliar ways. Anchor the chosen CARE tools to the existing ways of working for you and your team to lessen the energy required to make changes happen. Below we'll help you map the prompts to sustain determination.

Leveraging The 4Rs

When it comes to *often* investing in the actions that help build cultures of safety and care at the "Me", "We" and "Us" levels, our research has found CARE tools are best anchored into a workplace's daily rhythms of role modeling, rituals, routines, and rules. We call these the "4Rs" of culture.

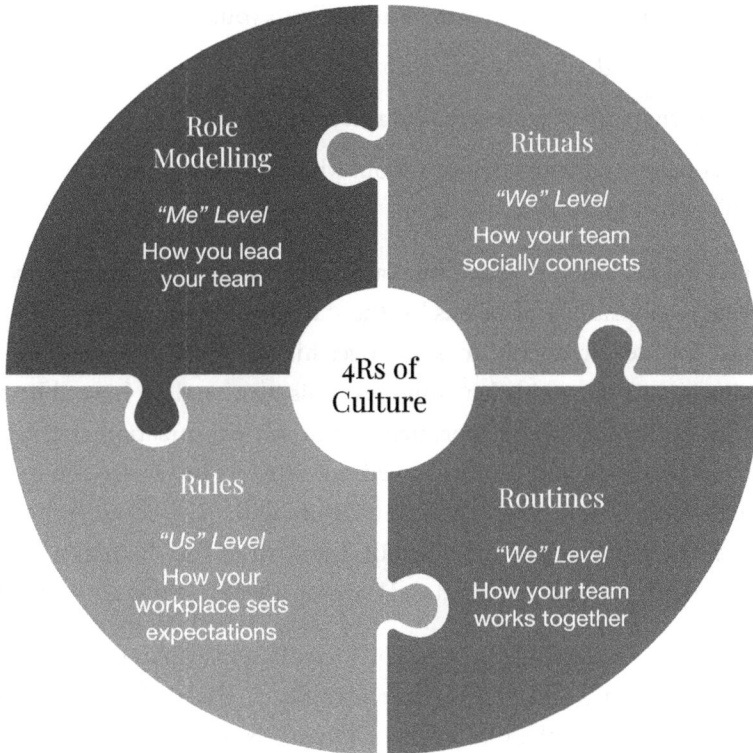

Figure 12: The "4Rs" Of Culture

"Me" Level Role Modelling: Being The Change We Want To See

Due to the influence we have as leaders in directing energy and resources within our teams, how we behave and where we focus our attention has a powerful impact on creating team norms. Culture change begins when we start to model the behaviour we want our teams to emulate.

For example, you can role model responsibility for your team when you:

* Don't pretend to have everything figured out;

* Are willing to ask your team for advice;

- Invite your team to co-create solutions with you;

- Follow through on your commitments;

- Take ownership of your setbacks and mistakes;

- Talk openly and with curiosity about what you are learning and how you can apply it to the next challenge.

Joel Gascoigne, CEO of social media platform Buffer, has repeatedly role modeled responsibility as he has led the start-up technology company over the past decade. He openly acknowledges his successes, his struggles, and his failures and shares his learnings with his team and on his public blog. These have included: his experiments with self-organization that left his team overwhelmed and lost; his failed investments in service innovations that led to cash flow problems and staff layoffs; and his co-founder disagreements that contributed to his burnout. From all of this, he notes: "Money will come and go, but experiences and learning is what I define as true wealth."

Joel also role models Buffer's values of "default to transparency", "focus on self-improvement", and "make time to reflect". His willingness to walk Buffer's talk is one of the reasons the company is repeatedly ranked as one of the best places to work in the technology industry.

"We" Level Rituals: Creating Spaces For Connection

Rituals are the informal practices teams use around significant events to build and sustain social cohesion and support a sense of belonging. They build feelings of safety and care as they help to communicate and build the skills to support the social norms valued in a workplace. For example, rituals may include new staff welcomes, fond farewells for people leaving, birthday morning teas, monthly lunch and learn sessions, time to volunteer in the community, opportunities to collaborate on passion projects, message boards to recognize and thank each other, "open mic" sessions to share stories, projects, or hobbies, and other team building activities. Our team's favorite is our "Friday Frolic" where we gather virtually for 30 minutes to catch up on anything other than the work we are doing.

An effective ritual creates a safe space for a team to socially connect in a more personal and meaningful way around their shared values. Rituals tap into our emotions to help build and reinforce social norms by giving permission to share specific beliefs, encourage certain actions, and reward desired behaviours. They draw attention to what is important, and function as communication and learning systems designed to shape the thoughts, feelings, and behaviours of team members. For example, the ritual of celebrating birthdays tells team members that their workplace cares and values each person individually and wants them to do the same for each other.

Why, when, where, how, and for whom rituals are enacted tends to be standardized and repetitive. For example, The Motley Fool — a financial services company that provides investment advice — have a carefully sequenced series of rituals to welcome new team hires with safety and care:

- A week before someone's first day, the hiring manager sends the new person a survey to complete on their interests, hobbies, investment experiences, and so on. This ritual communicates an interest in the whole person, not just their job skills.

- New hires always start on a Friday. When they arrive, their team has decorated the new person's desk with objects based on their survey responses. This might include favorite foods, favorite sports teams, and favorite pastimes. This ritual communicates the team's care and desire to welcome the new person.

- This is followed by a tour of the facilities, lunch with colleagues from other departments, a team party, and $100 to take friends or family out to dinner to celebrate the new job. New employees also receive stock in the company and $1,000 to invest (plus a six-week training program on how to analyze stocks and make investments). This ritual communicates the whole company's excitement to have the new person join them.

- On the first Monday, the new person is paired with a "buddy", who is a seasoned team member, to help them navigate the company, culture, processes, and systems. Over the first week, the buddy and team member jointly participate in a scavenger hunt that involves answering questions, solving riddles, and following clues—nudging the new hire to explore different parts of the company and to meet different people. This ritual communicates the organization's commitment to providing the new person with the support they need to do their job.

But the rituals at The Motley Fool don't just end with the warm welcome. Social rituals are continued with regularity including: Monthly "All-Fool" Activities (camping, theater, skiing, etc.), Birthday Celebration Day (first Friday of every month), Pizza Day (last Friday of every month), Mani-Pedi Day (once a month), Haircuts (once a month), and "Fooliversaries" (a celebration of each team member's hiring anniversary). Each ritual is designed to communicate the sense of care and belonging the organization has for its workers and encourages them to extend the same to each other.

"We" Level Routines: Getting The Work Done

Routines are the formal practices and processes teams use on a regular basis to get their work done. Common examples of routines include meetings, hiring routines, budgeting routines, and routines for providing services, producing products, and developing new products.

Far from being rigid and robotic, routines provide the safety guard rails for teams to more easily and effectively co-ordinate their efforts. When a team is familiar with a routine it helps them to get things done more quickly and reliably and leaves them with more time and energy for creativity and innovation.

For example, teams at Microsoft – a technology company – use the following routines to guide how they work together with safety and care:

- **Recharge Fridays** – People are encouraged to block off Fridays and use the time to focus on deep work and uninterrupted productivity. This means that no meetings are scheduled at this time. This routine supports the value of deep work and productivity.

- **Monthly Town Halls** – Every month, Microsoft holds an employee town hall meeting where company priorities, progress, and culture are discussed in an open forum. This meeting is broadcast live for employees around the globe and is also available on-demand for employees in other time zones. The leadership team provides a monthly business update and takes questions directly from the audience, as well as from their internal messaging platform Yammer. This routine supports open communication and learning.

- **Discover Days** – Microsoft employees are given access to a broader set of career opportunities and make themselves visible to the internal talent marketplace. This routine supports growth opportunities and talent retention.

- **OneWeek Hackathon** – Every year, Microsoft hosts a week-long event where employees from around the world – engineers, marketers, etc. – come together to share ideas, work on innovative projects, and collaborate on new initiatives. When they arrive, the race is on to sell their ideas to anyone who will listen. Reactions range from polite questions to vigorous debate and challenges. In the end, votes sent from smartphones are tallied, projects evaluated, winners celebrated. A few projects even receive funding as new business efforts. This routine supports learning and innovation and improves connection and collaboration across Microsoft.

"Us" Level Rules: Clearly Communicating Expectations

Rules are the written expectations that workplaces have established to guide people's behaviour. They are designed to provide structure, ensure fairness, comply with laws and standards, and ensure consistency in decision-making processes and operational procedures. Typically, rules are documented in codes of conduct, people management policies and processes, health, safety and wellbeing guides, and grievance complaints procedures among others.

Researchers have found that most workplaces create formal rules around conducting business in a truthful manner, protecting the environment, disclosing relevant information, keeping accurate records, respecting human rights, protecting health and safety, and contributing to society. Many of these formal rules are legal requirements – like the psychosocial legislation in Australia – designed to protect customers, employees, and communities from the risks that arise in workplaces.

While well intended, studies suggest that formal workplace rules are often misunderstood, ignored, and broken due to their poor design and implementation. And, even when people do their best to follow these rules, the unnecessary "red tape" they often add to people's workloads has been found to have a negative impact on performance. This has led more and more workplaces to look for ways to simplify their rules and ensure they are easy to follow by making them:

- **Memorable** – If people forget the rule, then they'll have forgotten the culture.

- **Meaningful** – Rules must answer the question "Why does this matter?" to clearly explain the cultural concept.

- **Common** – People must encounter the rule regularly. If a memorable rule applies only to situations people face once a year, it's more likely to become irrelevant.

For example:

- **Basecamp's "No Red Tape Expense Account" Rule** – Employees can spend "within reason" on any work-related expenses they require to do their jobs using their company credit card.

- **Microsoft's "Two Pizza" Rule** – Teams should be small enough to be fed by two pizzas.

- **Netflix's "No Vacation" Rule** – Employees can take as much vacation time as they want, as long as they get their work done and it doesn't affect the company's operations.

- **Shopify's "Just Say No To Meetings" Rule** – Workers are encouraged to scrap recurring meetings with more than three people in attendance. Meetings of any sort held on Wednesdays are out too, and any event with an invite list of over 50 people can only be held on Thursdays between 11am and 5pm.

- **Patagonia's "Let My People Go Surfing" Rule** – Employees are encouraged to take time off to enjoy the outdoors and pursue their passions, as part of their commitment to promoting work-life balance.

To be clear these workplaces haven't simply eliminated formal rules required of them by law. Even Netflix, whose culture is known for balancing freedom and responsibility and whose CEO wrote a book titled "No Rule Rules", still has a formal code of conduct. However, what these organizations are doing is making their rules easier to remember and follow in an effort to shape cultural norms that support safety and care.

Mindful Moment: The "4Rs" can provide a useful scaffold to support the development of your "Dynamic Map" to build and sustain a culture of safety and care. You can do this using the following final three steps:

- **Review Existing Investments:** Using your evaluation reflections from Part II, what are the safety and CARE strengths of your current leadership, team, and workplace approaches that you've identified? Note down on your "Dynamic Map":

    - *Your role modelling* – what values, mindsets, and behaviours do you already model that you want your team to emulate?

    - *The rituals* – what informal rituals do your team already use to socially connect around these shared values, mindsets, and behaviours?

    - *The routines* – what formal practices and processes do your team use on a regular basis to get work done?

    - *The rules* – what policies or procedures has your workplace established to help people feel safe and cared for?

        Remember that frequency matters, so add how frequently these investments in safety and CARE are occurring next to each item. Use: R = "Rarely", S = "Sometimes", O = "Often".

- **Close The Gaps:** Using your evaluation reflections from Part II, what are the psychosocial risks and CARE gaps your "Dynamic Map" may still have that need to be minimized or eliminated? If gaps exist, consider:

    - *Expand existing investments* – might some of the existing activities you've mapped have more impact if they happened more frequently?

        If yes, put a circle around these and update the desired frequency (R = "Rarely", S = "Sometimes", O = "Often").

- *Make new investments* – might a new activity be required to close an existing gap? Our studies have found that while leaders rely heavily on rules, a healthy culture of safety and care is more likely when there are investments in all "4Rs". You may already know what needs to be added and/or you may choose to add actions from the CARE Toolbox you've created. Just remember it's best to start small and frequent with a new action, rather than big and rarely. And, it's best to begin with no more than two or three new actions, and then add more once these are embedded. That's why the map is "dynamic" instead of static.

  When you're clear what action/s could help you close the safety and CARE gaps, draw a circle on your "Dynamic Map", note the action inside, and add the desired frequency (R = "Rarely", S = "Sometimes", O = "Often").

- **Step Back:** Review the "Dynamic Map" you've created and first ask yourself, and then ask your team:

  - Do the chosen priorities make sense based on the data gathered?

  - Are the existing and new investments occurring frequently enough to minimize the psychosocial risks your team faces and to build the desired culture of safety and care?

  - Are the required resources available to execute the investments? Will additional support be needed? Do any of the investments need to be scaled back?

  - How can the "Dynamic Map" be used to shape daily actions?

  - When will the map be reviewed and updated?

Once these steps are completed, you're ready to accelerate forward on your journey to building a culture of safety and care.

Tracking Your Progress

As you begin implementing your chosen safety and care actions, it's important that you, in the words of systems researcher Meg Wheatley, "don't confuse order with control". Don't fall back on trying to "manage" your team, but instead we recommend planning tight and then hanging loose as you "care" for your complex and dynamic team.

Sustaining the determination for change requires ongoing energy and effort. One way we have found to help leaders do this successfully is to track and follow your own energy, and the energy of your team, for the actions and changes you're implementing. And the good news is you already have tools to do this:

- **Evaluation Insights** – In Chapter 3, we explored different evaluation tools that can be used to measure levels of safety and care in your team. While these tools were focused on your experiences as a leader, the questions can be incorporated into any existing survey tools you use for your team. Just remember, any data you gather is a snapshot of a moment in time. More important than any one number is using your "Running A Research Review" template to spot the patterns of strengths and struggles so you can continue learning together.

- **"The Safety Check Chat"** – This tool in Chapter 4 can be used for informal and formal conversations to assess: What's going well? Where are we struggling? What are we learning? And, what do we want to try next? Remember, the "Chat" can be brief, in the form of an informal catch-up, or can be used to structure a deeper dive into how the team is tracking with the actions and expectations from your "Safety & CARE Dynamic Map".

Not only does gathering this data help track progress and any required adjustments, but studies have also found that creating these feedback loops helps teams to sustain their energy for learning and change without burning themselves out.

Fanning The Change

As we've learned throughout this book, our brains are wired to seek out social rewards and avoid social pain. For this reason, researchers suggest that social emotions such as gratitude are like booster shots for individual and collective determination when it comes to sticking with and realizing our goals.

The essence of any strategy to cultivate gratitude is to appraise situations in ways that allow people to appreciate other's efforts, support, and kindness. Workplace researcher, Shawn Achor suggests that we can become "praise prisms" for the safety and care behaviours we want to grow by:

- Focusing on the processes, effort, and learning, not just the outcomes. (i.e. "I really appreciate how hard you worked on showing compassion for other team members.")

- Celebrating what's working. (i.e. "Thank you for taking ownership of that problem.")

- Emphasizing the collective efforts of people and not just the star performers. (i.e. "I really valued the way you each brought your strengths to this challenge.")

The real power of gratitude doesn't come only from its expression; it comes from its shaping of behaviour. Ultimately, studies have found that ongoing progress is nourished by acts of interpersonal support such as respect, recognition, encouragement, and opportunities for affiliation.

The Power Of Peer Coaching

Leading can be lonely. The dynamic and complex nature of fostering safety and care means we are never "won and done", and we strongly encourage leaders to share the journey they are navigating with trusted peers.

Studies have found that peer-to-peer leadership can be an effective approach to learning and creating change, as it provides support from others who get to know and care about us, as well as hold us accountable for the goals we've set. Groups of three – a triad – seem to work best, where each leader is given the opportunity to share what's working well, where they're struggling, what they're learning, and what they'll try next. Think of it as a peer-to-peer "Safety Check Chat".

It is not the expectation in these coaching triads that leaders will solve each other problems, but that they will simply ask questions, listen, and encourage each other as needed. As the leadership triad shares their safety and care experiences, opportunities, and challenges with each other, the group provides a safe and caring space for leaders' learning and growth, just by being present for each other.

The Safety & Care To Keep Learning Together

As we've discovered throughout this book, leading a team of people is not an easy task. But it is our heartfelt hope – now you have the knowledge and tools you need to LEAD the literacy, evaluation, activation, and determination required to build a culture of safety and care – that your efforts can be more effective and rewarding.

We are grateful every day to work alongside leaders – like yourself – who want to protect their team's mental health and promote their wellbeing by building and sustaining cultures of safety and care. We truly believe that the future of our planet depends on leaders being willing to learn, experiment, and share the kind of work you have done throughout this book.

Our team at The Leaders Lab don't claim to have all the answers for how we do this. As you've now seen, figuring out what works depends on more than simply a code or legislation for psychosocial safety. Although the current changes are helping to bring new focus and energy to the responsibilities of workplaces, in the end, success will depend on the commitment of leaders to stay curious, be brave, and to keep sharing experiences with each other. Each investment we make helps to accelerate more knowledge, inspire new practices, and makes it easier for leaders in workplaces around the world to tailor their safety and care approaches to their unique context.

We're honored that you've walked this part of your leadership journey with us. You can find more free resources and tools at www.theleaderslab.net. Please don't hesitate to reach out and let us know what impact – good, bad, and anything in between – what you've learned in this book is having for you and your team, so we can all keep learning and growing together.

After all, as Edgar Schein – one of the original psychological safety researchers – wisely said: "The only thing of real importance that leaders do is to create and manage culture. If you do not manage culture, it manages you, and you may not even be aware of the extent to which it is happening."

Acknowledgements

With our heartfelt thanks...

Much like leading a team, writing a book is not easy but when you have the support of good people all around you it is deeply joyful and rewarding. Whilst writing this book we have been blessed with the support of amazing people.

Our original research on which this book is based would not be possible without the intellectual generosity and rigorous insights of Peggy Kern, Mandy O'Neill, and Scott Donaldson who helped shape our research questions and supported our analysis. Every word in this book was lovingly debated, shaped, and edited by our incredible Leaders Lab team of Shirley Moana Duff, Simone Outterridge, Helen Vatzakis, Julie Weste, Katia Murphy, Carla Ford, and Naomi Hill, who challenged our thinking every day. Without the passion, commitment, and kindness of our business partners Martin Sucha and Danielle Jacobs to help create thriving workplaces, we would not have had the time, resources, or clients we needed to create it.

We have had the great pleasure and privilege over the last five years to interview so many of the workplace researchers who studies are featured throughout this book on our *Making Positive Psychology Work* podcast. Each one of them generously gave their time to share their findings in the hope of helping us all to lead better. Special thanks to Amy Edmondson, Jane Dutton, Margaret Wheately, Edgar Schein, Carol Dweck, Kristen Neff,

Barbara Fredrickson, Martin Seligman, Margaret Heffernan, Susan David, Kim Cameron, Adam Grant, Wayne Baker, Robert Biswas Diener, Gervase Bushe, Nick Epley, Robert Emmons, BJ Fogg, Christopher Kukk, Monica Worline, Dominic Price, Kathleen Cator, Valorie Burton, Scott Barry Kauffman, Nick Craig, Scott Barry Kauffman, Robert Quinn, Ryan Niemiec, Robert McGrath, Timothy Clarke, Russ Harris, Rasmus Hougaard, Peter Schein, Michael Bush, Jenn Lim, Patty McCord, Peter McGraw, Alex Linley, and Stewart Friedman.

We are also incredibly grateful to the leaders around the work who have helped to develop the new international psychosocial safety standards, national codes, and local legislation. Your advocacy and action to help create safer workplaces for all of us is truly appreciated.

We benefited hugely from conversations with the incredible team of employment lawyers at Minter Ellison who made the legal jargon of the codes and legislation accessible for us. In particular, Amanda Watts, Caitlin Ible, and Deanna McMaster thank you for your clear counsel and wise guidance to help us create healthier workplaces.

And to our families and friends who constantly look for the best in us – even when we're miles away again – thank you for helping us to be the positive change we dream of in this world.

References

Introduction

While popular management theories would like you to believe... Taylor, F. W. (1911). *The principles of scientific management.* New York, NY: Harper & Brothers.

As a result, studies have found that the most successful leaders... Cameron, K., J. E. Dutton., & Quinn, R.E. (2003). *Positive organizational scholarship: Foundations of a new discipline.* San Francisco, CA: Berrett-Koehler; Cameron, K. S., & Spreitzer, G. M. (2011). *The Oxford handbook of positive organizational scholarship.* New York, NY: Oxford University Press; Dutton, J. E., & Spreitzer, G. M. (2014). *How to be a positive leader: Small actions, big impact.* San-Francisco, CA: Berrett-Koehler Publishers.

Professor Linda Hill's longitudinal research on leaders... Hill, L. A., Tedards, E., Wild, J., & Weber, K. (2022, September 19). *What makes a great leader?* Harvard Business Review. https://hbr.org/2022/09/what-makes-a-great-leader

As many organization and systems change researchers... Pascale, R., Milleman, M., & Gioja, L. (2000). *Surfing the edge of chaos: The new art and science of management.* New York, NY: Crown Business; Meadows, D. (2008). *Thinking in systems.* White River Junction, VT: Chelsea Green; Owen, H. (2008). *Wave rider: Leadership for high performance in a self-organizing world.* San-Francisco, CA: Berrett-Koehler Publishers; Holman, P. (2010). *Engaging emergence: Turning upheaval into opportunity.* San Francisco, CA: Berrett-Koehler Publishers.

As Margaret Wheatley, author of the widely acclaimed... Wheatley, M. J. (1992). *Leadership and the new science: Discovering order in a chaotic world.* San Francisco, CA: Berrett-Koehler Publishers.

This may help to explain why in May 2019... World Health Organization. (2019, May 28). *Burn-out an "occupational phenomenon": International Classification of Diseases.* https://www.who.int/news/item/28-05-2019-burn-out-an-occupational-phenomenon-international-classification-of-diseases

A growing list of countries are advocating... Cobb, E. P. (2022). *Managing psychosocial hazards and work-related stress in today's work environment: International insights for US organizations.* New York, NY: Taylor & Francis.

Part I

Researchers suggest that when we lack the language... Gergen, K. J. (1999). *An invitation to social construction.* Thousand Oaks, CA: Sage Publications Inc.

Neuroscientists have found that the regions our brains use... Atzil, S., Gao, W., Fradkin, I., & Barrett, L. F. (2018). Growing a social brain. *Nature Human Behaviour,* 2(9), 624-636.

As Dr. Brené Brown notes, language is... Brown, B. (2021). *Atlas of the heart: Mapping meaningful connection and the language of human experience.* New York, NY: Random House.

Chapter 1

Studies are absolutely clear that anything that contributes to chronic stress... Barrett, L. F. (2020). *Seven and a half lessons about the brain.* New York, NY: Harper Collins.

For example, in Australia between 2014 and 2018... NSW Government. (2020). *Tell us what you think about a psychological health code of practice.* https://www.haveyoursay.nsw.gov.au/draft-code-psychological-health

In Australia, since 2017 workers' compensation claims... Allianz Australia Insurance Limited. (2020). *Future thriving workplaces report.* https://www.allianz.com.au/images/internet/allianz-au/ContentImages/Allianz_Future%20Thriving%20Workplaces%20report.pdf

With the costs of psychosocial injuries and lost productivity starting to add up... European Agency for Health and Safety at Work. (2014). *Calculating the cost*

of work-related stress and psychosocial risks: European risk observatory literature review. https://www.researchgate.net/publication/323142494_Calculating_the_cost _of_work-related_stress_and_psychosocial_risks

The World Health Organization notes… World Health Organization. (2019, May 28). *Burn-out an occupational phenomenon: International Classification of Diseases.* https://www.who.int/news/item/28-05-2019-burn-out-an-occupational-phenom enon-international-classification-of-diseases

First used as a term in the 1970s by psychologist… Freudenberger, H. J. (1974). Staff burn-out. *Journal of Social Issues,* 30(1), 159-165.

Caused by an ongoing imbalance between the demands… Davis, P. (2021). *Beating burnout at work: Why teams hold the secret to well-being and resilience.* Pennsylvania, PA: Wharton School Press.

Studies have found it is most often experienced by people… Moss, J. (2019, December 11). *Burnout is about your workplace, not your people.* Harvard Business Review. https://hbr.org/2019/12/burnout-is-about-your-workplace-not-your-people

We can be experiencing burnout, without being burnt out… Malesic, J. (2022). *The end of burnout.* Oakland, CA: University of California Press.

Most of us are exposed to a combination of psychosocial hazards… Pinkos Cobb, E. (2022). *Managing psychosocial hazards and work-related stress in today's work environment.* Oxfordshire, UK: Taylor and Francis.

As far back as 1984, the International Labour Organization and World Health Organization… Joint ILO/WHO Committee on Occupational Health & International Labour Office. (1986). *Psychosocial factors at work: Recognition and control.* Geneva: International Labour Office. http://www.ilo.org/public/libdoc/ilo/ 1986/86B09_301_engl.pdf

In 2018, a study of 132 countries found that 47 countries… Chirico, F., Heponiemi, T., Pavlova, M., Zaffina, S., & Magnavita, N. (2019). Psychosocial risk prevention in a global occupational health perspective: A descriptive analysis. *International Journal of Environmental Research and Public Health,* 16(14), 2470.

Then, in 2021, the International Organization for Standardization… International Organization for Standardization. (2021). *Occupational health and safety management—Psychological health and safety at work—Guidelines for*

managing psychosocial risks. (ISO Standard No. 45003:2021). https://www.iso.org/obp/ui/#iso:std:iso:45003:ed-1:v1:en

Lawyer Ellen Pinkos Cobb in her book *Managing Psychosocial Hazards and Work-Related Stress in Today's Work Environment explains...* Pinkos Cobb, E. (2022). *Managing psychosocial hazards and work-related stress in today's work environment: International insights for US organizations.* New York, NY: Taylor & Francis.

The High Court in Australia recently awarded... Harrison, C. (2022, July 29). *Australia: Kozarov v Victoria: High court provides guidance on the scope and nature of the duty owed by employers to employees in psychiatric injury claim.* Mondaq. https://www.mondaq.com/australia/health-safety/1216342/kozarov-v-victoria-high-court-provides-guidance-on-the-scope-and-nature-of-the-duty-owed-by-employers-to-employees-in-psychiatric-injury-claim

Typically, the codes and legislation place the burden of responsibility on workplaces... Model Work Health and Safety Bill 2022 (Aus). https://www.safeworkaustralia.gov.au/safety-topic/managing-health-and-safety/mental-health/whs-duties/pcbu-duties

It is important to note that this is not an exhaustive list... International Organization for Standardization. (2021). *Occupational health and safety management—Psychological health and safety at work—Guidelines for managing psychosocial risks.* (ISO Standard No. 45003:2021). https://www.iso.org/obp/ui/#iso:std:iso:45003:ed-1:v1:en

Lower levels of engagement: Gallup estimate... Pendell, R. (2022, June 14). *The world's $7.8 trillion workplace problem.* Gallup. https://www.gallup.com/workplace/393497/world-trillion-workplace-problem.aspx

Increased absenteeism: Physical symptoms such as... Borritz, M., Rugulies, R., Christensen, K. B., Villadsen, E., & Kristensen, T. S. (2006). Burnout as a predictor of self-reported sickness absence among human service workers: Prospective findings from three year follow up of the PUMA study. *Occupational and Environmental Medicine, 63*(2), 98-106.; Gallup. (n.d.). *How to prevent employee burnout.* https://www.gallup.com/workplace/313160/preventing-and-dealing-with-employee-burnout.aspx

Increased compensation claims and medical expenses... Lynch, S. (2015, February 23). *Why your workplace might be killing you.* Stanford Graduate School of Business: Insights by Stanford Business. https://www.gsb.stanford.edu/insights/why-your-workplace-might-be-killing-you

Decreased productivity: Researchers have found... Harvard Health Publishing. (2021, February 15). *Protect your brain from stress.* https://www.health.harvard.edu/mind-and-mood/protect-your-brain-from-stress

One study in 2017 of over 17,000 employees... Mental Health America. (2017). *Mind the workplace.* https://mhanational.org/sites/default/files/Mind%20the%20Workplace%20-%20MHA%20Workplace%20Health%20Survey%202017%20FINAL.pdf

Studies have found they are more likely to engage in negative behaviors... Grandey, A. A., Dickter, D. N., & Sin, H.P. (2004). The customer is not always right: Customer aggression and emotion regulation of service employees. *Journal of Occupational Health Psychology,* 9(2), 137-151.

Increased turnover: People are nearly three times... Gallup. (n.d.). *How to prevent employee burnout.* https://www.gallup.com/workplace/313160/preventing-and-dealing-with-employee-burnout.aspx

An American federal jury awarded $168 million in damages... McCoy, K. (2017, October 25). *Sexual harassment: Here are some of the biggest cases.* USA Today. https://www.usatoday.com/story/money/2017/10/25/sexual-harassment-here-some-biggest-cases/791439001/

Uber's poor handling of sexual harassment and work design complaints... Siddiqui, F. (2019, August 29). *Internal data shows Uber's reputation hasn't changed much since #DeleteUber.* The Washington Post. https://www.washingtonpost.com/technology/2019/08/29/even-after-ubers-ipo-long-shadow-deleteuber-still-looms/

To put this very real business challenges into perspective... Peart, N. (2019, November 5). *Making work less stressful and more engaging for your employees.* Harvard Business Review. https://hbr.org/2019/11/making-work-less-stressful-and-more-engaging-for-your-employees; Australian Human Rights Commission. (2010). *2010 workers with mental illness: A practical guide for managers.* https://humanrights.gov.au/our-work/1-mental-health-workplace#fn7

Psychosocial injuries also have a societal impact... Hall, G. B., Dollard, M. F., Tuckey, M. R., Winefield, A. H., & Thompson, B. M. (2010). Job demands, work-family conflict, and emotional exhaustion in police officers: A longitudinal test of competing theories. *Journal of Occupational and Organizational Psychology,* 83(1), 237-250; Poortman, A. R. (2005). How work affects divorce: The mediating role of financial and time pressures. *Journal of Family Issues,* 26(2), 168-195; Milner, A., Witt, K., Maheen, H., & LaMontagne, A. D. (2017). Access to means of suicide, occupation, and the risk of suicide: A national study over 12 years of coronial data. *BMC Psychiatry,* 17, 1-7; Bailey, T. S., Dollard, M. F., & Richards, P. A. (2015). A national standard for psychosocial safety climate (PSC): PSC 41 as the benchmark for low risk of job strain and depressive symptoms. *Journal of Occupational Health Psychology,* 20(1), 15.

In 2008 the annual cost to society... European Agency for Health and Safety at Work. (2014). *Calculating the cost of work-related stress and psychosocial risks: European risk observatory.*

Patagonia has always been clear... Chuinard, Y. (2016). *Let my people go surfing.* London, UK: Penguin Books.

Patagonia is regularly listed on "best place to work... Rock, D. (2020, 9 January). *Patagonia's Dean Carter on how to treat employees like people.* [Audio podcast] *The NLI Interview.* https://www.forbes.com/sites/davidrock/2020/01/09/the-nli-inter view-patagonias-dean-carter-on-how-to-treat-employees-like-people/?sh=43a48 b36188c

Chapter 2

The US Surgeon General's workplace mental health... Murthy, V. (2022). *The US surgeon general's framework for workplace mental health and well-being.* U.S. Department of Health & Human Services. https://www.hhs.gov/surgeongeneral/ priorities/workplace-well-being/index.html#:~:text=Conclusion%20%26%20Next %20Steps-,The%20Surgeon%20General's%20Framework%20for%20Work place%20Mental%20Health%20and%20Well,any%20size%2C%20across%20 any%20industry.

Because studies have found that our performance depends on our ability to collaborate and learn alongside each other... Dweck, C. (2014). How companies can profit from a" growth mindset". *Harvard Business Review,* 92(11), 7.

Studies have found that the fear of appearing foolish or incompetent in front of other people... Lieberman, M. D. (2013). *Social: Why our brains are wired to connect.* New York, NY: Crown.

Fortunately, researchers have found that our brains fear of learning can be overcome... Schein E.H. (1993). How can organizations learn faster? The challenge of entering the green room. *Sloan Management Review,* 34:85-92

The key is having what Professor Amy Edmondson describes as... Edmondson A.C. (1996). Learning from mistakes is easier said than done: group and organizational influences on the detection and correction of human error. *Journal of Applied Behavior Science,* 32(1):5-28

More than sixty years of research has found that psychological safety... Newman, A., Donohue, R., & Eva, N. (2017). Psychological safety: A systematic review of the literature. *Human Resource Management Review,* 27(3), 521-535; Frazier, M. L., Fainshmidt, S., Klinger, R. L., Pezeshkan, A., & Vracheva, V. (2017). Psychological safety: A meta-analytic review and extension. *Personnel Psychology,* 70, 113-165.

Often defined as a "set of taken-for granted beliefs... Edmondson, A. C. (2018). *The fearless organization: Creating psychological safety in the workplace for learning, innovation, and growth.* Hoboken, NJ: John Wiley & Sons.

A longitudinal study by Google's People Analytics Unit... Duhigg, C. (2016). What Google learned from its quest to build the perfect team. *The New York Times Magazine,* 26.

Studies have found that when we treat each other with respect and care it calms our brain's threat system... Lieberman, M. D. (2013). *Social: Why our brains are wired to connect.* New York, NY: Crown.

Of course, neither Google or other researchers are suggesting that psychological safety guarantees... Nembhard, I. M., & Edmondson, A. C. (2011). Psychological safety: A foundation for speaking up, collaboration, and experimentation. In K. S. Cameron & G. M. Spreitzer (Eds.), *The oxford handbook of positive organizational scholarship. New York, NY:* Oxford University Press.

Dr. Amy Edmondson's suggests that psychological safety is best viewed... Edmondson, A. C., & Lei, Z. (2014). Psychological safety: The history, renaissance, and future of an interpersonal construct. *Annual Review of Organizational Psychology and Organizational Behavior,* 1(1), 23-43.

Studies have found we need to individually learn and practice the skills of... Edmondson, A. C., & Lei, Z. (2014). Psychological safety: The history, renaissance, and future of an interpersonal construct. *Annual Review of Organizational Psychology and Organizational Behavior,* 1(1), 23-43.

Because who we are... Tynan, R. (2005). The effects of threat sensitivity and face giving on dyadic psychological safety and upward communication. *Journal of Applied Social Psychology,* 35(2), 223-247.

MIT professors Edgar Schein and Warren Bennis found... Schein E.H., & Bennis W. (1965). *Personal and Organizational Change Through Group Methods.* New, York, NY: Wiley.

We propose that 'personal portable psychological safety'... Williams, P. (2022). *Becoming antifragile: Learning to thrive through disruption, challenge and change.* Toronto, OT: Grammar Factory Publishing.

Knowing we are in an organization that cares for us... Lieberman, M. D. (2013). *Social: Why our brains are wired to connect.* New York, NY: Crown

Dr. Mandy O'Neill's research in workplaces has found... McQuaid, M. (2020, 22 May). *Can you create a workplace with more love & connection with Mandy O'Neill* [Audio podcast]. Making Positive Psychology Work. https://www.michellemcquaid. com/podcast/can-you-create-a-workplace-with-more-love-connection-podcast-with-mandy-oneill/; O'Neill, O. A., Barsade, S. G., & Sguera, F. (2023). The psychological and financial impacts of an emotional culture of anxiety and its antidote, an emotional culture of companionate love. *Social Science & Medicine,* 317, 115570.

Studies have found that worker's perception of organizational support mediates... Carmeli, A., & Zisu, M. (2009). The relational underpinnings of quality internal auditing in medical clinics in Israel. *Social Science & Medicine,* 68(5), 894-902.

Psychological safety is fragile... Edmondson, A. C. & Hugander, P. (2021, June 22). *4 steps to boost psychological safety at your workplace.* Harvard Business Review. https://hbr.org/2021/06/4-steps-to-boost-psychological-safety-at-your-work place

Our data has found workers are more likely to report higher levels of every wellbeing factor... The Leaders Lab (2022). *The Leaders Lab Australia 2022 workplace report: The state of psychosocial safety in Australian workplaces.* https://

leaders-lab.s3.amazonaws.com/MMcQ_LeadersLab_Australia_Workplace_Report
_2019-2022.pdf

As Dr. Martin Seligman points out for more than half a century psychologists were focused on the study of mental illness... Seligman, M. E. (2002). Authentic happiness: Using the new positive psychology to realize your potential for lasting fulfillment. New York, NY: Simon and Schuster.

Studies have found that opportunities to experience engagement, meaning, accomplishment and positive emotion... McQuaid, M. & Kern, M.P. (2018). Your wellbeing blueprint: How to feel good & do well at work. Victoria, Australia: The Michelle McQuaid Group.

As the World Health Organization notes: "Health is a state... World Health Organization (1946). *Constitution of The World Health Organization.* https://www.who.int/about/governance/constitution

Other studies have found that 93% of Australian workers say their physical... Deloitte (2022). *Making Fair Work Flex Work.* https://www2.deloitte.com/au/en/pages/risk/articles/making-fair-work-flexwork.html

Because, while our data found that one-in-five Australian workers reported often experiencing feelings of burnout... The Leaders Lab (2022). *The Leaders Lab Australia 2022 workplace report: The state of psychosocial safety in Australian workplaces.* https://leaders-lab.s3.amazonaws.com/MMcQ_LeadersLab_Australia_Workplace_Report_2019-2022.pdf

Dr. Brené Brown notes: "Language is the greatest tool for meaningful connection... Brown, B. (2021). Atlas of the heart: Mapping meaningful connection and the language of human experience. New York, NY: Random House.

Part II

Researchers have found the more frequently we experience a sense of progress... Amabile, T., & Kramer, S. (2011). *The progress principle: Using small wins to ignite joy, engagement, and creativity at work.* Boston, MA: Harvard Business Press.

Chapter 3

In a world of constant change, we are neurologically wired... Kashdan, T. (2010). *Curious?: Discover the missing ingredient to a fulfilling life.* New York, NY: Harper Perennial.

Rather than face the reality that even the best equipped forecasters... Heffernan, M. (2020). *Uncharted: How to navigate the future.* New York, NY: Simon & Schuster.

Studies have found that the most effective leaders let go of their addition to prediction... Heffernan, M. (2020). *Uncharted: How to navigate the future.* New York, NY: Simon & Schuster.

As Peter Drucker, one of the greatest scholars of leadership and management... Drucker, P. F. (1966). *The effective executive* (1st ed.). New York, NY: HarperBusiness.

The challenge is that our brains are wired with a negativity bias... Baumeister, R. F., Bratslavsky, E., Finkenauer, C., & Vohs, K. D. (2001). Bad is stronger than good. *Review of General Psychology,* 5(4), 323-370.

When it comes to gathering, analyzing, and actioning data in workplaces researchers estimate... Cooperrider, D. L., & Godwin, L. N. (2011). Positive organization development: Innovation-inspired change in an economy and ecology of strengths. In K.S. Cameron, & G.M. Spreitzer (Eds.), *The Oxford handbook of positive organizational scholarship,* (pp. 73 -750). New York, NY: Oxford University Press.

The truth is that neither workplaces, leaders or teams can excel... Cooperrider, D.L., & McQuaid, M. (2012). The positive arc of systemic strengths: How appreciative inquiry and sustainable designing can bring out the best in human systems. *The Journal of Corporate Citizenship,* 2012(46), 71-102.

Chapter 4

As systems researcher Dr. Margaret Wheatley shares... Wheatley, M. J. (2009). *Turning to one another: Simple conversations to restore hope to the future.* San Francisco, CA: Berrett-Koehler Publishers, Inc.

Studies have found that teams who can engage each other in healthy conflict... Rock, D., Grant, H., & Grey, J. (2016). Diverse teams feel less comfortable–and that's why they perform better. *Harvard Business Review.* https://hbr.org/2016/09/diverse-teams-feel-less-comfortable-and-thats-why-they-perform-better

To overcome these obstacles, MIT Professor Edgar Schein suggests... Schein, E. H., & Schein, P. A. (2018). *Humble leadership: The power of relationships, openness, and trust.* San Francisco, CA: Berrett-Koehler Publishers.

When we separately stumbled across the research of Professor David Cooperrider... Cooperrider, D., Whitney, D. D., & Stavros, J. M. (2000). *The appreciative inquiry handbook: For leaders of change.* San-Francisco, CA: Berrett-Koehler Publishers.

Changing our behaviors is hard... Kotter, J. P. (2012). *Leading change.* Boston, MA: Harvard Business Press.

Appreciative inquiry is an action-based research methodology... Cooperrider, D. (2017) "The gift of new eyes: Personal reflections after 30 years of appreciative inquiry in organizational life." In, Shani, A.B., & Noumair, D.A. (Eds.) *Research in organizational change and development,* Volume 25. Bingley UK: Emerald Publishing.

In fact, studies suggest that many people come away from these conversations... Bushe, G. R., & Kassam, A. F. (2005). When is appreciative inquiry transformational? A meta-case analysis. *The Journal of Applied Behavioral Science,* 41(2), 161-181.

Researchers have found that instead of seeking to control the outcomes... Owen, H. (2008). *Wave rider: Leadership for high performance in a self-organizing world.* San-Francisco, CA: Berrett-Koehler Publishers.

Part III

Studies have found the activities likely to be the most effective for your team will depend on the psychosocial risks... Newman, A., Donohue, R., & Eva, N. (2017). Psychological safety: A systematic review of the literature. *Human resource management review,* 27(3), 521-535.

As Peter Drucker noted: "The task of leadership... Drucker, P. F. (1966). *The effective executive.* (1st ed.). New York, NY: Harper Business.

Professors Edward Deci and Richard Ryan (2008) have found across more than thirty years of research... Ryan, R. M., & Deci, E. L. (2017). *Self-determination theory: Basic psychological needs in motivation, development, and wellness.* New York, NY: Guilford Press.

Chapter 5

Researchers have found that our brains have a tendency to fluctuate between self-serving distortions and ruthless self-criticism... Neff, K. (2011). *Self-compassion: The proven power of being kind to yourself.* London, UK; Hachette.

For example, studies have found that many of us think we're funnier... Alicke, M. D., & Govorun, O. (2005). The better-than-average effect. In M. D. Alicke, D. A. Dunning & J. I. Krueger (Eds.), *The Self in Social Judgment.* (pp. 85-106). New York: Psychology Press.

In addition to over-estimating our own abilities... Alicke, M. D., & Sedikides, C. (2009). Self-enhancement and self-protection: What they are and what they do. *European Review of Social Psychology,* 20, 1-48.

The truth is that while self-aggrandizing and self-judgmental behaviors... Neff, K. D. (2011). Self-compassion, self-esteem, and well-being. *Social and personality psychology compass,* 5(1), 1-12.

Closely aligned with Dr. Kristen Neff's research on self-compassion... Neff, K. D. & Dahm, K. A. (2015). Self-Compassion: What It Is, What It Does, and How It Relates to Mindfulness. *In Handbook of Mindfulness and Self-Regulation* (pp. 121-137). New York, NY: Springer.

Studies have found these self-soothing behaviors... Gilbert, P., & Procter, S. (2006). Compassionate mind training for people with high shame and self-criticism: Overview and pilot study of a group therapy approach. *Clinical Psychology & Psychotherapy: An International Journal of Theory & Practice,* 13(6), 353-379.

Given the actions and emotions of leaders have been found to be contagious... Barsade, S., & O'Neill, O. A. (2016). Manage your emotional culture. *Harvard Business Review,* 94(1), 58-66.

This triggers a variety of physiological and neurological processes that causes them to 'catch' their leader's anxiety... Barsade, S. G. (2002). The ripple effect:

Emotional contagion and its influence on group behavior. *Administrative Science Quarterly,* 47(4), 644-675.

Studies have found that both negative and positive emotions are contagious between leaders and their teams... Barsade, S. G., Coutifaris, C. G., & Pillemer, J. (2018). Emotional contagion in organizational life. *Research in Organizational Behavior,* 38, 137-151.

Studies have found that the expression of self-compassion activates our brain's caregiving... Neff, K. (2011). *Self-compassion: The proven power of being kind to yourself.* London, UK; Hachette.

Sometimes this requires comforting ourselves as we lean into uncomfortable emotions... Neff, K. D. (2023). Self-compassion: Theory, method, research, and intervention. *Annual Review of Psychology,* 74, 193-218

Hit Your Reset Button... McQuaid, M. (2017, August 19). *Can you cultivate self-compassion with Dr. Kristen Neff* [Audio podcast]. Making Positive Psychology Work. https://www.michellemcquaid.com/podcast/mppw55-kristin-neff/

Watch Your Language... McQuaid, M. (2019, August 16). *Are you being sucked into a negativity vortex with Dr. Ethan Cross* [audio podcast]. Making Positive Psychology Work. https://www.michellemcquaid.com/podcast/are-you-being-sucked -into-a-negativity-vortex-podcast-with-ethan-kross/

Take A Time Out... Neff, K. D. & Davidson, O. (2016). Self-compassion: Embracing suffering with kindness. In I. Ivtzan & T. Lomas (Eds.), *Mindfulness in Positive Psychology* (pp. 37-50). Rutledge.

Own Your Stuff... McQuaid, M. (2017, February 17). *Practicing acceptance commitment therapy with Dr. Russ Harris* [audio podcast]. Making Positive Psychology Work. https://www.michellemcquaid.com/podcast/mppw-32-russ-harris/

Find Your Mantra... McQuaid, M. (2017, January 20). *Can self-compassion kick start your motivation with Kathleen Cator* [audio podcast]. Making Positive Psychology Work. https://www.michellemcquaid.com/podcast/mppw-30-kathleen-cator/

In contrast, having our strengths – the things we are good at and enjoy doing... Buckingham, M. & Clifton, D. O. (2001). *Now, Discover Your Strengths.* New York, NY: Simon and Schuster.

It is the state psychologists call "flow"... Csikszentmihalyi, M. (1990). *Flow: The Psychology of Optimal Experience.* New York, NY: Harper Perennial.

Discover Your Strengths... McQuaid, M. & Lawn, E. (2014). *Your Strengths Blueprint: How to be Engaged, Energized & Happy at Work.* Melbourne, Victoria: Michelle McQuaid Pty Ltd.

Check Your Blind Spots... Niemiec, R. M., & McGrath, R. E. (2019). *The power of character strengths: Appreciate and ignite your positive personality.* Cincinnati, OH: VIA Institute on Character.

Find A Tah-Dah... McQuaid, M. (2017, August 25). *Can you put your strengths to work with Dr. Ryan Neimiec* [audio podcast]. Making Positive Psychology Work. https://www.michellemcquaid.com/podcast/dr-ryan-niemiec/

Craft Your Job... Berg, J. M., Dutton, J. E. & Wrzesniewski, A. (2013). Job crafting and meaningful work. *Purpose and Meaning in the Workplace,* 81-104.

Run An Appreciation Lap... DeSteno, D. (2018). *Emotional success: The power of gratitude, compassion and pride.* New York, NY: Houghton Mifflin Harcourt Publishing.

Studies suggest that on average most of us spend at least thirty minutes... Wakeman, C. (2017). *No ego: How leaders can cut the cost of workplace drama, end entitlement, and drive big results.* New York, NY: St. Martin's Griffin.

Professor Carol Dweck's research has found that people who willingly take responsibility... Dweck, C. (2006). *Mindset: The new psychology of success.* New York, NY: Random House.

Studies suggest that when we practice a growth mindset... McQuaid, M. (2017, April 14). *Does your workplace have a growth mindset with Dr. Carol Dweck* [audio podcast]. Making Positive Psychology Work. https://www.michellemcquaid.com/podcast/mppw42-carol-dweck/

Practicing a growth mindset makes it easier for us to take responsibility... Dweck, C. (2016). What having a "growth mindset" actually means. *Harvard Business Review,* 13(2), 2-5.

Remind Yourself Not Yet... Dweck, C. (2014). The power of believing that you can improve. TED Talk. Transcript and video available: https://www.ted.com/talks/

carol_dweck_the_power_of_believing_that_you_can_improve/transcript

Leave Your Comfort Zone… Kay, K. & Shipman, C. (2014). *The Confidence Code: The Science and Art of Self-Assurance: What Women Should Know.* New York, NY: Harper Collins.

Find The Gift… McQuaid, M. (2016, December 16). *Can you get comfortably uncomfortable with Dr. Robert Biswas-Diener* [audio podcast]. Making Positive Psychology Work. https://www.michellemcquaid.com/podcast/mppw26-robert-biswas-diener/

Ask For Help… McQuaid, M. (2019, November 29). *Do you need to ask for more help with Dr. Wayne Baker* [audio podcast]. Making Positive Psychology Work. https://www.michellemcquaid.com/podcast/do-you-need-to-ask-for-help-more-podcast-with-wayne-baker/

Confess Your Screw Ups… McQuaid, M. (2018, June 1). *Can you build psychological safety with Dr. Amy Edmondson* [audio podcast]. Making Positive Psychology Work. https://www.michellemcquaid.com/podcast/can-build-psychological-safety/

Researcher Dr. Susan David explains that our emotions… David, S., & Congleton, C. (2013). Emotional agility. *Harvard Business Review,* 91(11), 125-131.

Proactively prioritizing opportunities to experience positive emotions… McQuaid, M. (2016, December 30). *What good are positive emotions with Dr. Barbara Fredrickson* [audio podcast]. Making Positive Psychology Work. https://www.michellemcquaid.com/podcast/what-good-are-positive-emotions-podcast-with-barbara-fredrickson/

Researchers have found that developing distress tolerance… Kashdan, T. & Biswas-Diener, R. (2014). *The Upside of Your Dark Side: Why Being Your Whole Self—Not Just Your "Good" Self—Drives Success and Fulfillment.* New York, NY: Penguin.

Take A Joy Break… Garland, E. L., Fredrickson, B., Kring, A. M., Johnson, D. P., Meyer, P. S. & Penn, D. L. (2010). Upward spirals of positive emotions counter downward spirals of negativity: Insights from the broaden-and-build theory and affective neuroscience on the treatment of emotion dysfunctions and deficits in psychopathology. *Clinical Psychology Review,* 30(7), 849-864.

Ask What The Func?... McQuaid, M. (2018, June 29). *Do you need more emotional agility with Dr. Susan David* [audio podcast]. Making Positive Psychology Work. Group. https://www.michellemcquaid.com/podcast/need-emotional-agility-podcast-susan-david/

Step Back To Step Forward... McQuaid, M. (2018, July 27). *Can you be commercial and compassionate with Dr. Rasmus Hougaard* [audio podcast]. Making Positive Psychology Work. https://www.michellemcquaid.com/podcast/can-you-be-comm ercial-and-compassionate-podcast-with-rasmus-hougaard/

Navigate Negativity Landmines... Fredrickson, B.L. (2009). Positivity: *Ground-breaking Research Reveals How to Embrace the Hidden Strength of Positive Emotions, Overcome Negativity, and Thrive.* New York, NY: Random House.

Slow Down Your Responses... McQuaid, M. (2020, May 8). *Do you need to choose between self-sacrifice and self-development with Dr. Scott Barry Kauffman* [audio podcast]. Making Positive Psychology Work. https://www.michellemcquaid.com/podcast/do-you-need-to-choose-between-self-sacrifice-self-development-podcast-with-dr-scott-kauffman/

Chapter 6

We all share the same deep psychological needs... Peterson, C. (2006). *A primer in positive psychology.* New York, NY: Oxford University Press.

Studies have found that even when people we don't know well characterize us as "dependable"... Izuma, K., Saito, D. N., & Sadato, N. (2008). Processing of social and monetary rewards in the human striatum. *Neuron, 58(2),* 284-294.

Studies show that each positive interaction helps to return the cardiovascular system... Heaphy, E., & Dutton, J. E. (2008). Positive social interactions and the human body at work: Linking organizations and physiology. *Academy of Man-agement Review, 33,* 137–162; Theorell, T., Orth-Gomér, K., & Eneroth, P. (1990). Slow-reacting immunoglobin in relation to social support and changes in job strain: A preliminary note. *Psychosomatic Medicine, 52,* 511-516.

Studies have found that people with strong relationships at work... Heaphy, E., & Dutton, J. E. (2008). Positive social interactions and the human body at work: Linking organizations and physiology. *Academy of Management Review, 33,* 137-162.

Researchers have found that when our relationships at work are strained... Dutton, J. E. (2003). *Energize your workplace: How to create and sustain high-quality connections at work.* San Francisco, CA: John Wiley & Sons.

One study of over 350 employees in sixty business units at a financial services company found.. Campion, M. A., Papper, E. M., & Medsker, G. J. (1996). Relations between work team characteristics and effectiveness: A replication and extension. *Personnel Psychology, 49,* 429-452.

Neuroscientist Lisa Barrett Feldman notes... Barrett, Lisa Feldman. (2020). *Seven and a half lessons about the brain.* New York, NY: HarperCollins.

Studies suggest that the amount of time we spend collaborating with others... Cross, R., Arena, M., Pryor G., Hinds, R., & Bowman, T. (2022). How to fix collaboration overload. *Harvard Business Review.* Retrieved from: https://hbr.org/2022/12/how-to-fix-collaboration-overload

Researchers have found we tend to do better in groups than we do individually... Medina, J. (2022). *Brain rules for work: The science of thinking smarter in the office and at home.* Seattle, WA: Pear Press.

Some studies suggest many groups consistently underperform... Hackman, J. R., & Hackman, R. J. (2002). *Leading teams: Setting the stage for great performances.* Boston, MA: Harvard Business Press; Cross, R., Arena, M., Pryor G., Hinds, R., & Bowman, T. (2022). How to fix collaboration overload. *Harvard Business Review.* Retrieved from: https://hbr.org/2022/12/how-to-fix-collaboration-overload.

Researchers have found that as we interact, on an almost minute-to-minute basis... Lieberman, M. D. (2013). *Social: Why our brains are wired to connect.* New York, NY: Crown.

People tend to over-estimate our mind reading abilities... Epley, N. (2015). *Mindwise: Why we misunderstand what others think, believe, feel, and want.* New York, NY: Vintage.

Researchers suggest the only way to minimize this neurological risk in our teams... Epley, N., & Eyal, T. (2019). Through a looking glass, darkly: Using mechanisms of mind perception to identify accuracy, overconfidence, and underappreciated means for improvement. In *Advances in experimental social psychology* (Vol. 60, pp. 65-120). Academic Press.

As workplace researcher Dr. Gervase Bushe explains... McQuaid, M. (2018, February 2). *Is this common mistake ruining your relationships with Dr. Gervase Busche* [Audio podcast]. Making Positive Psychology Work. https://www.michelle mcquaid.com/podcast/podcast-nick-epley/

Researchers suggest the only way to minimize this neurological risk... McQuaid, M. (2018, October 5). *Do your leaders have the right mindset with Dr. Nicholas Epley* [Audio podcast]. Making Positive Psychology Work. https://www.michellemcquaid. com/podcast/leaders-right-mindset-podcast-gervase-bushe/

Dr. Brené Brown suggests starting with the belief that most of the time... Brown, B. (2017). *Rising strong: How the ability to reset transforms the way we live, love, parent, and lead.* New York, NY: Random House.

Studies have found that caring for team members is the most important thing leaders can do... McQuaid, M. (2021, July 9). *Can you create a great place to work with Michael Bush* [Audio podcast]. Making Positive Psychology Work. https:// www.michellemcquaid.com/podcast/can-you-create-a-great-place-to-work/

Researchers suggest that this experience of power propels us forward... Keltner, D. (2016). *The power paradox: How we gain and lose influence.* New York, NY: Penguin.

Our actions as leaders communicate what is expected and acceptable for our teams... Tyler, T. R., & Lind, E. A. (1992). A relational model of authority in groups. In M. P. Zanna (Ed.), *Advances in experimental social psychology,* (Vol. 25, pp. 115-191). Academic Press.

Studies have found leaders can have a significant impact on their team's levels of psychological safety... Deci, E. L., Olafsen, A. H., & Ryan, R. M. (2017). Self-determination theory in work organizations: The state of a science. *Annual Review Of Organizational Psychology And Organizational Behavior,* 4, 19-43; Nembhard, I. M., & Edmondson, A. C. (2006). Making it safe: The effects of leader inclusiveness and professional status on psychological safety and improvement efforts in health care teams. *Journal of Organizational Behavior: The International Journal of Industrial, Occupational and Organizational Psychology and Behavior,* 27(7), 941-966.; Edmondson, A. C., & Lei, Z. (2014). Psychological safety: The history, renaissance, and future of an interpersonal construct. *Annual Review Organi-zational Psychology Organizational Behavior,* 1(1), 23-43.

For psychological safety to exist in your team, there must be a shared belief... Frazier, M. L., Fainshmidt, S., Klinger, R. L., Pezeshkan, A., & Vracheva, V. (2017). Psychological safety: A meta-analytic review and extension. *Personnel Psychology,* 70(1), 113-165.

This is especially true when team members hold varying levels of authority and influence... Edmondson, A. (2003). Managing the risk of learning: Psychological safety in work teams. In M. West, D. Tjosvold & K. Smith (Eds.), *International handbook of organizational teamwork and cooperative work* (pp. 255-275). London: Wiley.

The team level, psychological safety is more than just the trust one person... Edmondson, A. C., Kramer, R. M., & Cook, K. S. (2004). Psychological safety, trust, and learning in organizations: A group-level lens. *Trust and distrust in organizations: Dilemmas and approaches,* 12(2004), 239-272.

Dr. Jane Dutton and her colleagues have found when our interactions... Carmeli, A., Brueller, D., & Dutton, J. E. (2009). Learning behaviors in the workplace: The role of high-quality interpersonal relationships and psychological safety. Systems Research and Behavioral Science: *The Official Journal of the International Federation for Systems Research,* 26(1), 81-98.

If we apply the research to any given context, it is likely that every day someone in your team is struggling... Kanov, J. M., Maitlis, S., Worline, M. C., Dutton, J. E., Frost, P. J. & Lilius, J. M. (2004). Compassion in organizational life. *American Behavioral Scientist,* 47(6), 808-827.

Studies have found that the most compassionate people also set the most effective boundaries... Brown, B. (2018). *Dare to lead: Brave work. Tough conversations. Whole hearts.* New York, NY: Random House.

Studies have found that compassion is a four-part process... Worline, M., Dutton, J. E., & Sisodia, R. (2017). *Awakening compassion at work: The quiet power that elevates people and organizations.* Oakland, CA: Berrett-Koehler Publishers.

Get Curious... Etheve, M. (2020, December 4). *Are you a humble leader with Dr. Edgar Schein and Dr. Peter Schein* [Audio podcast]. Making Positive Psychology Work. https://www.michellemcquaid.com/podcast/are-you-a-humble-leader-podcast-with-edgar-peter-schein/

Use Code Lavender Alerts... Zak, P. (2022). *Trust factor: The science of creating high-performance companies*. New York, NY: Harper Collins.

Embrace Diversity... McQuaid, M. (2020, June 12). *Do you practice racial empathy with Valorie Burton* [Audio podcast]. Making Positive Psychology Work. https://www.michellemcquaid.com/podcast/do-you-practice-racial-empathy-podcast-with-valorie-burton/

Share Opposing Views... McQuaid, M. (2018, February 16). *Is employee engagement over rated with Patty McCord* [Audio podcast]. Making Positive Psychology Work. https://www.michellemcquaid.com/podcast/employee-engage ment-rated-podcast-patty-mccord/

Drink Coffee Together... McQuaid, M. (2019, April 12). *Is a competitive spirit killing your workplace with Dr. Margaret Heffernan* [Audio podcast]. Making Positive Psychology Work. https://www.michellemcquaid.com/podcast/competitive-spirit-killing-workplace-podcast-dr-margaret-heffernan/

Studies have found that levels of engagement, performance, sense of safety, and wellbeing... Clifton, D. O., & Harter, J. K. (2003). Investing in strengths. In K. S. Cameron, J. E. Dutton, & R. E. Quinn (Eds.), *Positive organizational scholarship* (pp. 111-121). San Francisco, CA: Berrett-Koehler.

Using these strengths at work has been found to improve levels of job resources... Linley, P. A. (2008). *Average to A+: Realizing strengths in yourself and others*. Coventry, UK: CAPP Press.

Leave us feeling more energized, creative, confident, and resilient... Buckingham, M. & Clifton, D. O. (2001). *Now, Discover Your Strengths*. New York, NY: Simon and Schuster.

Researchers have cautioned that this can make people more vulnerable... Biswas-Diener, R., Kashdan, T. B., & Minhas, G. (2011). A dynamic approach to psychological strength development and intervention. *The Journal of Positive Psychology*, 6(2), 106-118.

Share Strengths... McQuaid, M. (2017, November 3). *Are you underusing your strengths with Dr. Robert McGrath* [Audio podcast]. Making Positive Psychology Work. https://www.michellemcquaid.com/podcast/podcast-with-robert-mcgrath/

Co-Create Job Titles... McQuaid, M. (2018, April 13). *Do you need a happiness business model with Jenn Lim* [Audio podcast]. Making Positive Psychology Work. https://www.michellemcquaid.com/podcast/need-happiness-business-model-podcast-jenn-lim/

Give Strengths-Feedback... Spreitzer, G., & Porath, C. (2012). Creating sustainable performance. *Harvard Business Review,* 90(1), 92-99.

Have A Strengths Check... Buckingham, M., & Goodall, A. (2015). Reinventing performance management. *Harvard Business Review,* 93(4), 40-50.

Navigate Strengths Collisions... Niemiec, R. M., & McGrath, R. E. (2019). *The power of character strengths: Appreciate and ignite your positive personality.* Cincinnati, OH: VIA Institute on Character.

When it comes to taking responsibility, studies have found that most people struggle with accountability... Partners In Leadership (2014). *Accountability: The low-hanging fruit for optimizing individual and organizational performance.* https://www.slideshare.net/MikaNurmesniemi1/workplace-accountability-study

Research has shown there are five factors that influence the likelihood of someone taking responsibility... Han, Y. & Perry, J. L. (2020). Conceptual bases of employee accountability: A psychological approach. *Perspectives on Public Management and Governance,* 3(4), 288-304.

Take A Purposeful Pause... McQuaid, M. (2020, May 8). *Do you need to choose between self-sacrifice and self-development with Dr. Scott Barry Kauffman* [audio podcast]. Making Positive Psychology Work. https://www.michellemcquaid.com/podcast/do-you-need-to-choose-between-self-sacrifice-self-development-podcast-with-dr-scott-kauffman/

Ask SMARTly... McQuaid, M. (2019, November 29). *Do you need to ask for more help with Dr. Wayne Baker* [audio podcast]. Making Positive Psychology Work. https://www.michellemcquaid.com/podcast/do-you-need-to-ask-for-help-more-podcast-with-wayne-baker/

Build A Boundaries Checklist... Brown, B. (2018). *Dare to lead: Brave work. Tough conversations. Whole hearts.* New York, NY: Random House.

Share The Victory Laps... O'Malley, M. & Baker, W.F. (2020). *Organizations for people caring cultures, basic needs, and better lives.* Stanford, California: Stanford University Press.

Talk To People, Not About People... McQuaid, M. (2018, February 16). *Is employee engagement overrated with Patty McCord* [Audio podcast]. Making Positive Psychology Work. https://www.michellemcquaid.com/podcast/employee-engagement -rated-podcast-patty-mccord/

Neuroscientist Dr. Uri Hasson's studies have found that when we connect with someone... Hasson, U., & Frith, C. D. (2016). Mirroring and beyond: coupled dynamics as a generalized framework for modelling social interactions. *Philosophical Transactions of the Royal Society B: Biological Sciences,* 371(1693), 20150366.

Pleasant mood contagion in teams has been associated with greater co-operation... Barsade, S. G. (2002). The ripple effect: Emotional contagion and its influence on group behavior. *Administrative Science Quarterly,* 47(4), 644-675.

Respond Actively And Constructively... King, L. A. (2001). The health benefits of writing about life goals. *Personality and Social Psychology Bulletin,* 27(7), 798-807.

Monitor Your Signals... McQuaid, M. (2019, November 8). *Do you know the four stages of psychological safety with Timothy Clarke* [audio podcast]. Making Positive Psychology Work. https://www.michellemcquaid.com/podcast/do-you-know-the- 4-stages-of-psychological-safety-podcast-with-tim-clark/

Broaden Each Other's Perspectives... McQuaid, M. (2019, August 16). *Are you being sucked into a negativity vortex with Dr. Ethan Cross* [audio podcast]. Making Positive Psychology Work. https://www.michellemcquaid.com/podcast/are-you- being-sucked-into-a-negativity-vortex-podcast-with-ethan-kross/

Invest In Favors... McQuaid, M. (2017, July 28). *Are you an effective giver with Dr. Adam Grant* [audio podcast]. Making Positive Psychology Work. https://www. michellemcquaid.com/podcast/mppw058-adam-grant/

Ignite Gratitude... McQuaid, M. (2020, July 24). *Are you reaching for gratitude at work with Dr. Robert Emmons* [audio podcast]. Making Positive Psychology Work. https://www.michellemcquaid.com/podcast/are-you-reaching-for-gratitude-at- work-podcast-with-robert-emmons/

Chapter 7

Studies have repeatedly found that healthy workplace cultures foster employee commitment... Sackmann, S. A. (2011). Culture and performance. In N. M. Ashkanasy, C. P. Wilderom., & M. F. Peterson. (Eds.). *Handbook of organizational culture and climate,* (2nd ed., pp. 188-224). Thousand Oaks, CA: SAGE Publications.

Data-driven financial analysts acknowledge culture is a critical factor... Kotter, J.P., & Heskett, J.L. (1992). *Corporate culture and performance.* New York, NY: Free Press.

Seventy-eight percent of Fortune 1000 CEO's and CFO's view culture... Graham, J. R., Harvey, C. R., Popadak, J., & Rajgopal, S. (2016). *Corporate culture: Evidence from the field.* SSRN paper. http://ssrn.com/abstract=2805602

Culture is the glue that binds the ways we work together... Cameron, K. S., Quinn, R. E., DeGraff, J., & Thakor, A. V. (2022). *Competing values leadership.* Northhampton, MA: Edward Elgar Publishing.

Studies have found that because culture is a product of accumulative beliefs, values, norms, and practices it is never static... Chatman, J. A., & O'Reilly, C. A. (2016). Paradigm lost: Reinvigorating the study of organizational culture. *Research in Organizational Behavior,* 36, 199-224.

Culture is also shaped by what is unfolding in the world around our workplaces... Sackmann, S. A. (2011). *Success factor: Corporate culture: Developing a corporate culture for high performance and long-term competitiveness, six best practices.* Gütersloh, North Rhine-Westphalia; Verlag Bertelsmann Stiftung.

Dr. Jennifer Chatman and her colleagues suggest healthy cultures... Chatman, J. A., & O'Reilly, C. A. (2016). Paradigm lost: Reinvigorating the study of organizational culture. *Research in Organizational Behavior,* 36, 199-224.

Studies have found workplaces who develop healthy cultures regardless of their age, size, or industry, consistently share one value... Chatman, J. A., & Cha, S. E. (2003). Leading by leveraging culture. *California Management Review,* 45(4), 20-34.

For example, luxury department store Nordstrom is famous for its culture of outstanding customer service... Solomon, M. (2016). What any business can learn from Nordstrom customer service. *Forbes.* https://www.forbes.com/sites/micah

solomon/2016/01/26/what-any-business-can-learn-from-the-way-nordstrom-handles-customer-service/?sh=18ad43f55b9e

Studies suggest that one of the most effective ways to encourage the norms of safety and caring across our workplaces... Newman, A., Donohue, R., & Eva, N. (2017). Psychological safety: A systematic review of the literature. *Human Resource Management Review, 27(3), 521-535.*

Researchers have found that when human resource practices signal a workplace's long-term investment in a mutually respectful relationship with its people... Collins, C. J., & Smith, K. G. (2006). Knowledge exchange and combination: The role of human resource practices in the performance of high-technology firms. *Academy Of Management Journal, 49(3), 544-560.*

The brain lights up with pleasure when we co-operate... Lieberman, M. D. (2013). *Social: Why our brains are wired to connect.* New York, NY: Crown.

The values and norms of a workplace have been found to be more effective at controlling behaviors... Chatman, J. A., & Cha, S. E. (2003). Leading by leveraging culture. *California Management Review, 45(4), 20-34.*

Our Nordstrom customer didn't start out having an exceptional experience... Chatman, J. A., & Cha, S. E. (2003). Leading by leveraging culture. *California Management Review, 45(4), 20-34.*

Strong norms increase our clarity about priorities and expectations as well as our bonds with one another... Grant, A. (2022). *The four deadly sins of work culture* [audio podcast]. WorkLife with Adam Grant. https://www.ted.com/podcasts/worklife/the-4-deadly-sins-of-work-culture-transcript

Australian software company Atlassian is known for its unique and innovative approach to collaboration, transparency, and employee empowerment... Price, D. (2022). What does a culture of innovation really look like? *Atlassian Work Life.* https://www.atlassian.com/blog/inside-atlassian/how-to-build-culture-of-innovation-every-day

The company's founders, employees, and stakeholders came together and agreed a shared set of values... Rogers. B. (2017). How culture drives Atlassian's ambitions to be the collaboration platform for all companies. *Forbes.* https://www.forbes.com/sites/brucerogers/2017/01/20/how-culture-drives-atlassians-ambitions-to-be-the-collaboration-platform-for-all-companies/?sh=2e81a4016f41

For example, it's structure... Culture of Business (2019). Atlassian's 3 most important company culture secrets (and how they used them to build their billion-dollar business). *CUB Blog.* https://cub.club/blog/atlassians-3-most-important-company-culture-secrets-and-how-they-used-them-to-build-their-billion-dollar-business/

Atlassian recruits leaders who demonstrate its values of openness, honest and collaboration... McQuaid, M. (2020, September 18). *Can you improve the health & performance of your team with Dominic Price* [audio podcast]. Making Positive Psychology Work. https://www.michellemcquaid.com/podcast/can-you-improve-the-health-performance-of-your-team-podcast-with-dominic-price/

Studies suggest that over time competition undermines our performance... McQuaid, M. (2017, December 8). *Is compassion the key to success with Dr. Christopher Kukk* [audio podcast]. Making Positive Psychology Work. https://www.michellemcquaid.com/podcast/is-compassion-the-key-to-success-podcast-with-chris-kukk/

Researchers have found that while we all may be competitive to some extent, we also need high levels of trust and helpfulness... Kukk, C. L. (2017). *The compassionate achiever: How helping others fuels success.* New York, NY: HarperCollins.

It turns the most productive workplaces are characterized by giving... Podsakoff, N. P., Whiting, S. W., Podsakoff, P. M., & Blume, B. D. (2009). Individual- and organizational-level consequences of organizational citizenship behaviors: A meta-analysis. *Journal of Applied Psychology,* 94(1), 122–141.

Organizational researcher Dr. Adam Grant explains that while people are inherently generous... Grant, A. (2013). In the company of givers and takers. *Harvard Business Review,* 91(4), 90-97.

Studies have found that when a culture of generosity is prioritized people are more efficient... Grant, A. (2013). *Give and take: A revolutionary approach to success.* New York NY: Penguin.

Be Purpose Driven... McQuaid, M. (2019, February 8). *Is purpose your compass at work with Nick Craig* [audio podcast]. Making Positive Psychology Work. https://www.michellemcquaid.com/podcast/purpose-compass-work-podcast-nick-craig/

Invest In Values... Brown, B. (2018). *Dare to lead: Brave work. Tough conversations. Whole hearts.* New York, NY: Random House.

Ask For Help... McQuaid, M. (2019, November 29). *Do you need to ask for more help with Dr. Wayne Baker* [audio podcast]. Making Positive Psychology Work. https://www.michellemcquaid.com/podcast/do-you-need-to-ask-for-help-more-podcast-with-wayne-baker/

Make Helping Fun... McQuaid, M. (2019, November 29). *Do you need to ask for more help with Dr. Wayne Baker* [audio podcast]. Making Positive Psychology Work. https://www.michellemcquaid.com/podcast/do-you-need-to-ask-for-help-more-podcast-with-wayne-baker/

Encourage Kindness... O'Malley, M. & Baker, W.F. (2020). *Organizations for people caring cultures, basic needs, and better lives.* Stanford, California: Stanford University Press.

Studies have found that when workplaces believe in focusing on their people's strengths... Harter, J. K., Schmidt, F. L., & Hayes, T. L. (2002). Business-unit-level relationship between employee satisfaction, employee engagement, and business outcomes: A meta-analysis. *Journal of Applied Psychology, 87,* 268-279.

Researchers suggest that human resources practices like job design, role descriptions... Van Woerkom, M., & Meyers, M. C. (2015). My strengths count! Effects of a strengths-based psychological climate on positive affect and job performance. *Human Resource Management, 54*(1), 81-103.

Studies suggest a strengths-focused human resources practices need to support... McQuaid, M. (2019). *The Strengths Lab 2019 workplace survey: The impact of putting our strengths to work.* The Michelle McQuaid Group. https://s3.amazonaws.com/MichelleMcQuaidWebsite/MMcQ_StrengthsLab_Workplace Survey2019.pdf

Coach Leaders... Harter, J. K., Schmidt, F. L., & Hayes, T. L. (2002). Business-unit-level relationship between employee satisfaction, employee engagement, and business outcomes: A meta-analysis. *Journal of Applied Psychology, 87,* 268–279.

Hire For Strengths... McQuaid, M. (2018, August 10). *Need a strengths energy boost with Dr. Alex Linley* [audio podcast]. Making Positive Psychology Work. https://www.michellemcquaid.com/podcast/need-strengths-energy-boost/

Redesign Jobs... Buckingham, M. (2022). Designing work that people love. *Harvard Business Review, 100*(5-6), 66-75.

Invest In Strengths Development... Buckingham, M. (2013). What if performance management focused on strengths? *Harvard Business Review, 3.*

Invite Flash Mentoring... Coyle, D. (2018). *The culture code: The secrets of highly successful groups.* New York, NY: Bantam Books.

Studies have found that the extent to which people perceive decisions to be fair... Lieberman, M. D. (2013). *Social: Why our brains are wired to connect.* New York, NY: Crown.

Researchers suggest that people are four times more likely to be honest... Carucci, D. (2020). How to actually encourage employee accountability. *Harvard Business Review.* https://hbr.org/2020/11/how-to-actually-encourage-employee-accountability

Researchers recommend building the following cultural norms for fairness and accountability... Bregman, P. (2016). The right way to hold people accountable. *Harvard Business Review.* https://hbr.org/2016/01/the-right-way-to-hold-people-accountable?ab=at_art_art_1x4_s01

Honor Commitments... Dela Rosa, C. (2021, December 14). *Do operating rhythms drive company culture?* [audio podcast] Work Check. https://www.atlassian.com/blog/podcast/work-check/season/season-1/do-operating-rhythms-drive-company-culture#takeaways

Confront Performance Problems... McQuaid, M. (2019, November 8). *Do you know the four stages of psychological safety with Timothy Clarke* [audio podcast]. Making Positive Psychology Work. https://www.michellemcquaid.com/podcast/do-you-know-the-4-stages-of-psychological-safety-podcast-with-tim-clark/

Get What You Pay For... McQuaid, M. (2019, October 25). *4 skills to improve your relationships at work with Dr. Jane Dutton* [audio podcast]. Making Positive Psychology Work. https://www.michellemcquaid.com/podcast/4-skills-to-improve-your-relationships-at-work-podcast-with-arne-carlsen/; Grant, A. (2022). *The four deadly sins of work culture* [audio podcast]. WorkLife with Adam Grant. https://www.ted.com/podcasts/worklife/the-4-deadly-sins-of-work-culture-transcript

Provide Air Cover... McQuaid, M. (2019, April 12). *Is a competitive spirit killing your workplace with Dr. Margaret Heffernan* [Audio podcast]. Making Positive Psychology Work. https://www.michellemcquaid.com/podcast/competitive-spirit-killing-workplace-podcast-dr-margaret-heffernan/

Audit Your Culture... Grant, A. (2022). *The four deadly sins of work culture* [audio podcast]. WorkLife with Adam Grant. https://www.ted.com/podcasts/worklife/the-4-deadly-sins-of-work-culture-transcript

Researchers have found that over time patterns of emotions tend to be repeated in teams... Ashkanasy, N. M., & Humphrey, R. H. (2011). Current emotion research in organizational behavior. *Emotion Review,* 3(2), 214-224.

Has also been found to help reduce anxiety and lower burnout... O'Neill, O. A., Barsade, S. G., & Sguera, F. (2023). The psychological and financial impacts of an emotional culture of anxiety and its antidote, an emotional culture of companionate love. *Social Science & Medicine,* 317, 115570.

Give What You Can... McQuaid, M. (2019, March 29). *Does your organization need an energy boost with Dr. Wayne Baker* [audio podcast]. Making Positive Psychology Work. https://www.michellemcquaid.com/podcast/organization-need-energy-boost-podcast-wayne-baker/

Celebrate Rites Of Passage... O'Malley, M. & Baker, W.F. (2020). *Organizations for people caring cultures, basic needs, and better lives.* Stanford, California: Stanford University Press.

Embrace Fun... McQuaid, M. (2018, February 9). *Is humor the key to improving relationships with Dr. Peter McGraw* [audio podcast]. Making Positive Psychology Work. https://www.michellemcquaid.com/podcast/humor-impact-wellbeing-podcast-peter-mcgraw/

Deliver Negative Stuff Personally... O'Malley, M. & Baker, W.F. (2020). *Organizations for people caring cultures, basic needs, and better lives.* Stanford, California: Stanford University Press.

Think About Others... McQuaid, M. (2020, September 18). *Can you improve the health & performance of your team with Dominic Price* [audio podcast]. Making Positive Psychology Work. https://www.michellemcquaid.com/podcast/can-you-improve-the-health-performance-of-your-team-podcast-with-dominic-price/

Part IV

When it comes to building a culture of safety and care our research has repeatedly found that it is the frequency... The Leaders Lab (2022). *The Leaders Lab Australia 2022 workplace report: The state of psychosocial safety in Australian workplaces.* https://leaders-lab.s3.amazonaws.com/MMcQ_LeadersLab_Australia _Workplace_Report_2019-2022.pdf

Chapter 8

Researchers have found that we tend to set goals that are too big... Fogg, B. J. (2019). *Tiny habits: The small changes that change everything.* Eamon Dolan Books.

Studies suggest these common challenges for creating behavior changes... McQuaid, M. (2019, November 15). *Do you need a tiny wellbeing habit with B.J. Fogg* [Audio podcast]. Making Positive Psychology Work. https://www.michelle mcquaid.com/podcast/do-you-need-a-tiny-wellbeing-habit-podcast-with-bj-fogg/

Joel Gascoigne, CEO of social media platform Buffer, has repeatedly role modeled responsibility... Gascoigne, J. (2020, December 3). *Reflecting on 10 years of building Buffer.* https://joel.is/10-years/

Repeatedly ranked as one of the best workplaces to work... Buffer. (2018, June 20). *Buffer named one of Inc. Magazine's best workplaces of 2018.* [Press release] https://buffer.com/press/inc-best-workplaces-2018

Rituals are the informal practices teams use around significant events to build and sustain social cohesion... Trice, H. M., & Beyer, J. M. (1993). *The cultures of work organizations.* New York, NY: Prentice-Hall, Inc.

An effective ritual creates a safe space for a team to socially connect... Smith, A. C., & Stewart, B. (2011). Organizational rituals: Features, functions and mechanisms. *International Journal of Management Reviews,* 13(2), 113-133.

The Motley Fool—a financial services and investment company — have a carefully sequenced series of rituals... O'Malley, M. & Baker, W.F. (2020). *Organizations for people caring cultures, basic needs, and better lives.* Stanford, California: Stanford University Press.

Routines are the formal practices and processes teams use on a regular basis... Feldman, M. S. (2000). Organizational Routines as a Source of Continuous Change. *Organization Science,* 11(6), 611-629.

Recharge Fridays... Singer-Velush, N., Sherman, K., & Anderson, E. (2020). Microsoft analyzed data on its newly remote workforce. *Harvard Business Review,* 15.

Monthly Town Halls... Hougaard, R., Carter, J., Hogan, K. (2019). How Microsoft builds a sense of community among 144,000 employees. *Harvard Business Review.* https://hbr.org/2019/08/how-microsoft-builds-a-sense-of-community-among-144000-employees

"Discover Days"... Carucci, R. & Hogan, K. (2022) 6 ways to reenergize a depleted team. *Harvard Business Review.* https://hbr.org/2022/11/6-ways-to-reenergize-a-depleted-team

OneWeek Hackathon... Nadella, S. (2018). *Hit refresh.* New York, NYL Harper Collins.

Rules are the written expectations your workplace has established... DeHart-Davis, L., Davis, R. S., & Mohr, Z. (2015). Green tape and job satisfaction: Can organizational rules make employees happy?. *Journal of Public Administration Research and Theory,* 25(3), 849-876.

Researchers have found that most workplaces create formal rules... Paine, L., Deshpandé, R., Margolis, J. D., & Bettcher, K. E. (2005). Up to code: Does your company's conduct meet world-class standards? *Harvard Business Review,* 83(12), 122-33.

The unnecessary "red tape" they often add to people's workloads has been found to have a negative impact on performance... Blom, R., Borst, R. T., & Voorn, B. (2021). Pathology or inconvenience? A meta-analysis of the impact of red tape on people and organizations. *Review of Public Personnel Administration,* 41(4), 623-650.

Basecamp "No Red Tape Expense Account"... Groth, A. (2017) This company trusts its employees so much it has a "no limits" expense policy. *Quartz.* https://qz.com/954675/this-company-trusts-its-employees-so-much-it-has-a-no-limits-expense-policy

Microsoft's "Two Pizza"... ET Bureau (2019). Nadella's 3-rule method, Bezos's 2-pizza team norm: How top bosses make meetings more productive. *The Economic Times.* https://economictimes.indiatimes.com/magazines/panache/nadellas-3-rule-method-bezoss-2-pizza-team-norm-how-top-bosses-make-meetings-more-produ ctive/lets-talk-business/slideshow/70869423.cms

Netflix's "No Vacation"... McCord, P. (2014). How Netflix reinvented HR. *Harvard Business Review,* 92(1), 71-76.

Shopify's "Just Say No To Meetings"... Demopoulos, A. (2023). The company purging meetings from calendars: 'Uninterrupted time is precious'. *The Guardian.* https://www.theguardian.com/money/2023/jan/06/work-meetings-shopify-isolation

Patagonia's "Let My People Go Surfing"... Clifford. C. (2016). The founder of Patagonia fishes half the year and tells his employees to go surfing. *CNBC Make It.* https://www.cnbc.com/2016/12/23/founder-of-patagonia-fishes-half-the-year-tells-his-employees-to-surf.html

Even Netflix whose culture is known for balancing freedom and responsibility... Marks, J.T. & Muruel, M. (2021, December 17). The story of internal controls and Netflix. [Blog] *Baker Tilly.* https://www.bakertilly.com/insights/the-story-of-internal-controls-and-netflix

The words of systems researcher Meg Wheatley, "we don't confuse order with control"... Wheatley, M. J. (1992). *Leadership and the new science: Discovering order in a chaotic world.* San-Francisco, CA: Berrett-Koehler.

Studies have found that creating these kinds of feedback loops... Senge, P. M. (1990). *The fifth discipline: The art & practice of the learning organization.* New York, NY: Doubleday.

Workplace researcher, Shawn Achor suggests that when we can become "praise prisms"... Achor. S. (2018). *Big potential: How transforming the pursuit of success raises our achievement, happiness, and well-being.* New York, NY: The Crown Publishing Group.

Studies have found that ongoing progress is nourished... Amabile, T., & Kramer, S. (2011). *The progress principle: Using small wins to ignite joy, engagement, and creativity at work.* Boston, MA: Harvard Business Press.

Studies have found that peer-to-peer leadership can be an effective approach to learning and creating change... McQuaid, M. (2020, March 6). *Are you feeling out of balance at work with Stewart Friedman* [Audio podcast]. Making Positive Psychology Work. https://www.michellemcquaid.com/podcast/are-you-feeling-out-of-balance-at-work-podcast-with-stewart-friedman/

As Edgar Schein - one of the original psychological safety researchers - wisely said: "The only thing of real importance that leaders do... Schein, E. H. (2010). *Organizational culture and leadership* (Vol. 2). New York, NY: John Wiley & Sons.

About The Authors

About Michelle McQuaid

Dr. Michelle McQuaid is a best-selling author, workplace wellbeing teacher, and playful change activator. With more than twenty years of senior leadership experience in small and large organizations around the world, she's passionate about translating cutting-edge research from human flourishing, into practical strategies to help leaders minimize psychosocial risks, build psychological safety, and create cultures of safety and care.

An honorary fellow at Melbourne University's Graduate School of Education, she blogs for Psychology Today and her work has been featured in Forbes, the Harvard Business Review, the Wall Street Journal, Boss Magazine, The Age and more. In 2022, she as recognized as one of LinkedIn's top 10 mental health experts.

She holds a Masters in Applied Positive Psychology from the University of Pennsylvania and completed her PhD in Appreciative Inquiry under the supervision of David Cooperrider.

Michelle lives to help people thrive, even in the midst of struggle. You can find more of Michelle's work at **www.michellemcquaid.com**.

About Paige Williams

Dr. Paige Williams is an author, researcher and PhD in Organizational Behaviour. A trusted advisor and mentor to senior leaders across business, government, education and beyond, she uses a potent blend of neuroscience, psychology and her own twenty-plus years of international business leadership experience to surface uncomfortable truths and help leaders see the rules they need to break in order to breakthrough and lead themselves, their teams, and their organizations to thrive.

The results are dramatic and measurable.

An Honorary Fellow of the Centre for Wellbeing Science and an Associate of Melbourne Business School, Paige is known as a leadership and culture expert. The potent combination of real-life leadership experience and deep academic knowledge fuels Paige's 'superpower' of translating complex ideas and academic research to make them real, relevant, and relatable to the work that leaders do every day. She has worked with thousands of leaders across business, government, NGOs, and education.

Paige's work has been featured in a variety of academic and non-academic journals including Psychology Today, Smart Company, Australian Financial Review and Human Resource Management and her latest book *Own It! Honouring and Amplifying Accountability* explores why accountability is the strategic imperative in the post-COVID economic landscape, and how we can be better at it.

www.ingramcontent.com/pod-product-compliance
Lightning Source LLC
Chambersburg PA
CBHW072102020426
42334CB00017B/1605